GREAT ESCAPES OF WORLD WAR II

BEHIND ENEMY LINES

THE ESCAPE OF ROBERT GRIMES WITH THE COMET LINE

by Matt Chandler

Raintree is an imprint of Capstone Global Library Limited, a company incorporated in England and Wales having its registered office at 264 Banbury Road, Oxford, OX2 7DY – Registered company number: 6695582

www.raintree.co.uk
myorders@raintree.co.uk

Editor: Christopher Harbo
Art Director: Nathan Gassman
Designer: Ted Williams
Media Researcher: Wanda Winch
Production Specialist: Gene Bentdahl
Illustrator: Dante Ginevra

ISBN 978 1 4747 3215 4 (hardback)
21 20 19 18 17
10 9 8 7 6 5 4 3 2 1

ISBN 978 1 4747 3219 2 (paperback)
22 21 20 19 18
10 9 8 7 6 5 4 3 2 1

British Library Cataloguing in Publication Data
A full catalogue record for this book is available from the British Library.

Design Element: Shutterstock: aodaodaodaod,
paper texture, esfera, map design,
Natalya Kalyatina, barbed wire design

CONTENTS

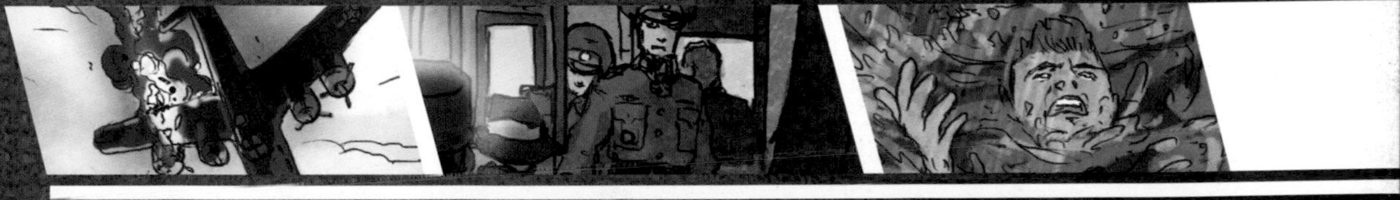

THE GREAT WAR

World War II (1939–1945) stands as the bloodiest war in human history. Somewhere between 50 and 70 million people died in a conflict that pitted the Allied forces against the Axis powers. The Allies consisted of Great Britain, France, the United States, the Soviet Union and many other nations. The Axis nations included Germany, Italy and Japan.

During the war, the Allies carried out millions of bombing sorties over Germany and Japan. Many of these missions were flown with B-17 bombers. These huge warplanes were nicknamed "Flying Fortresses", but they weren't impenetrable. On October 14 1943, the Allies lost 60 B-17 bombers and 600 men in a single day – a day that became known as Black Thursday.

Just six days after Black Thursday, US Army Lieutenant Robert Z. Grimes readied his own B-17 for battle. Grimes was a member of the US Army 8th Air Force 96th Bomb Group. His squadron had been bombing targets over Nazi-controlled Europe for weeks. Grimes and his crew of nine men had just returned from a vicious battle during which his plane was nearly shot down. Grimes had guided the crippled plane to safety, but on 20 October he was set to fly a new plane into battle.

Little did Grimes know, he and his crew would never complete their mission. By nightfall he found himself on the run from the Nazis. His only hope was a secret group of Resistance fighters known as the Comet Line.

THE LONG ROAD TO FREEDOM

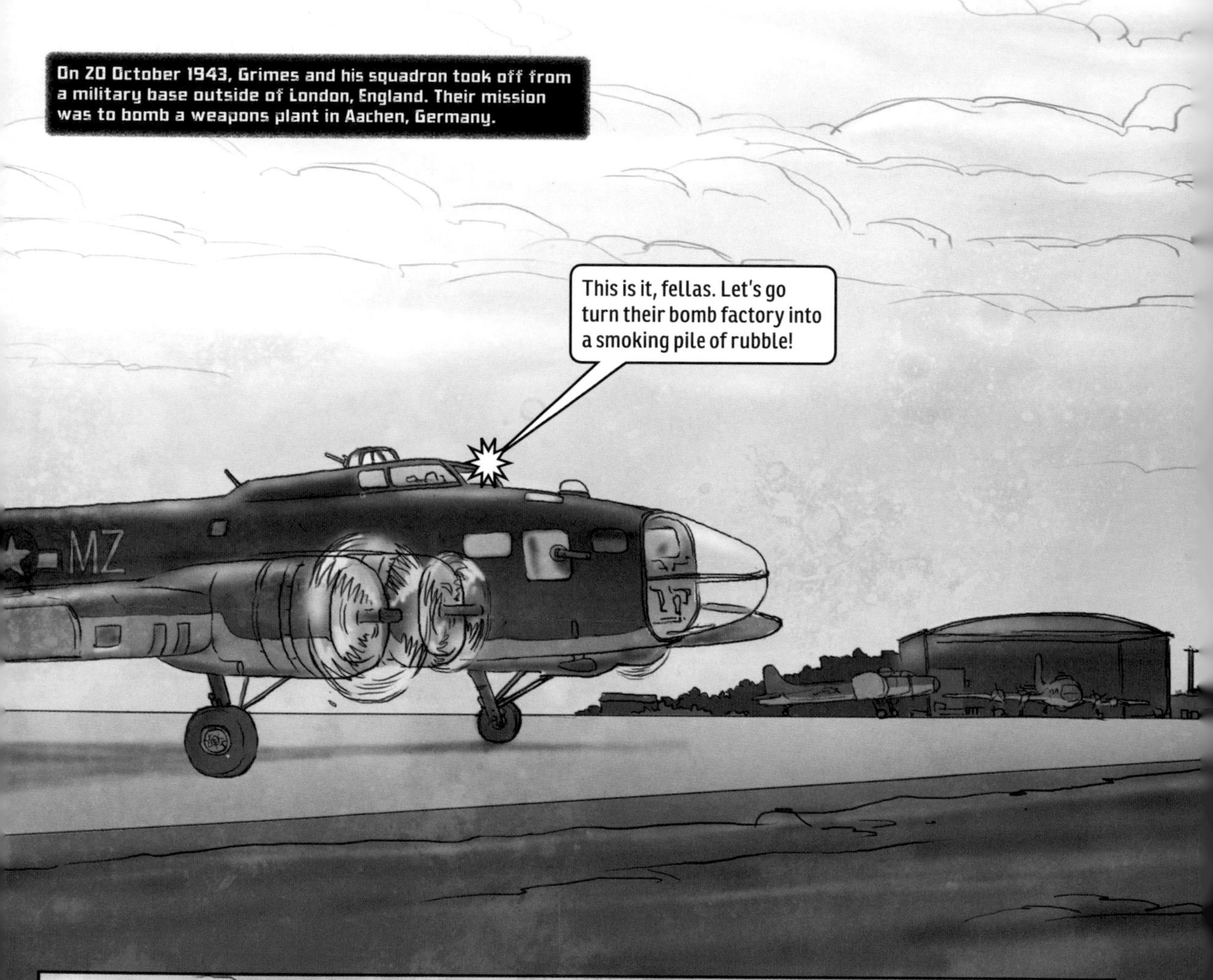
On 20 October 1943, Grimes and his squadron took off from a military base outside of London, England. Their mission was to bomb a weapons plant in Aachen, Germany.
This is it, fellas. Let's go turn their bomb factory into a smoking pile of rubble!
MZ

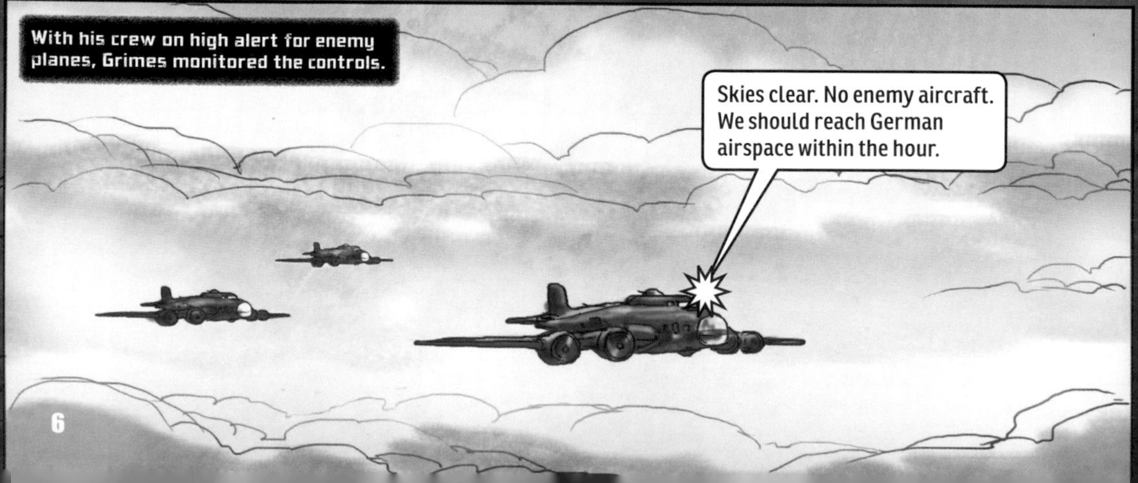
With his crew on high alert for enemy planes, Grimes monitored the controls.
Skies clear. No enemy aircraft. We should reach German airspace within the hour.

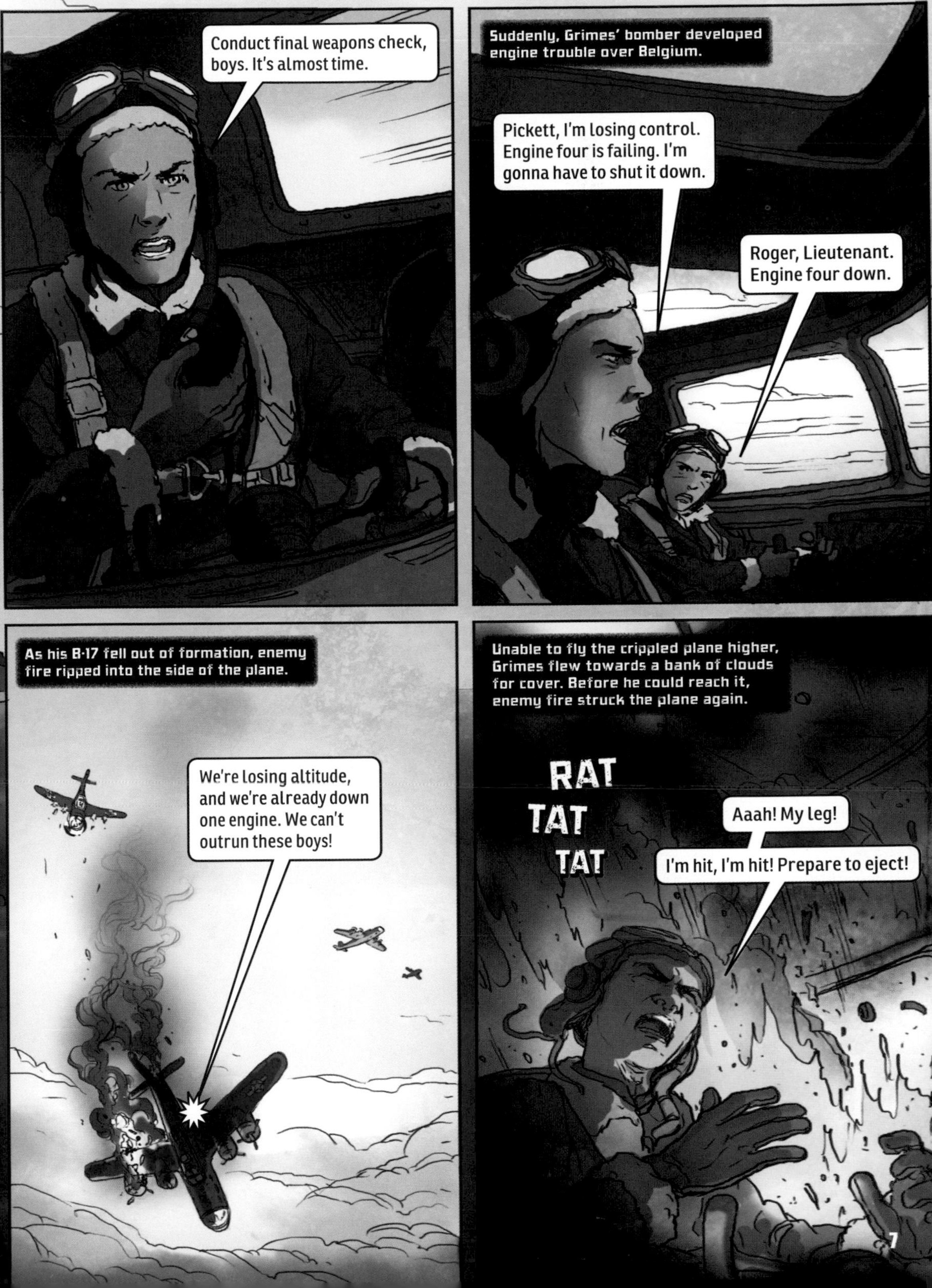
Conduct final weapons check, boys. It's almost time.
Suddenly, Grimes' bomber developed engine trouble over Belgium.
Pickett, I'm losing control. Engine four is failing. I'm gonna have to shut it down.
Roger, Lieutenant. Engine four down.
As his B-17 fell out of formation, enemy fire ripped into the side of the plane.
We're losing altitude, and we're already down one engine. We can't outrun these boys!
Unable to fly the crippled plane higher, Grimes flew towards a bank of clouds for cover. Before he could reach it, enemy fire struck the plane again.
RAT
TAT
TAT
Aaah! My leg!
I'm hit, I'm hit! Prepare to eject!

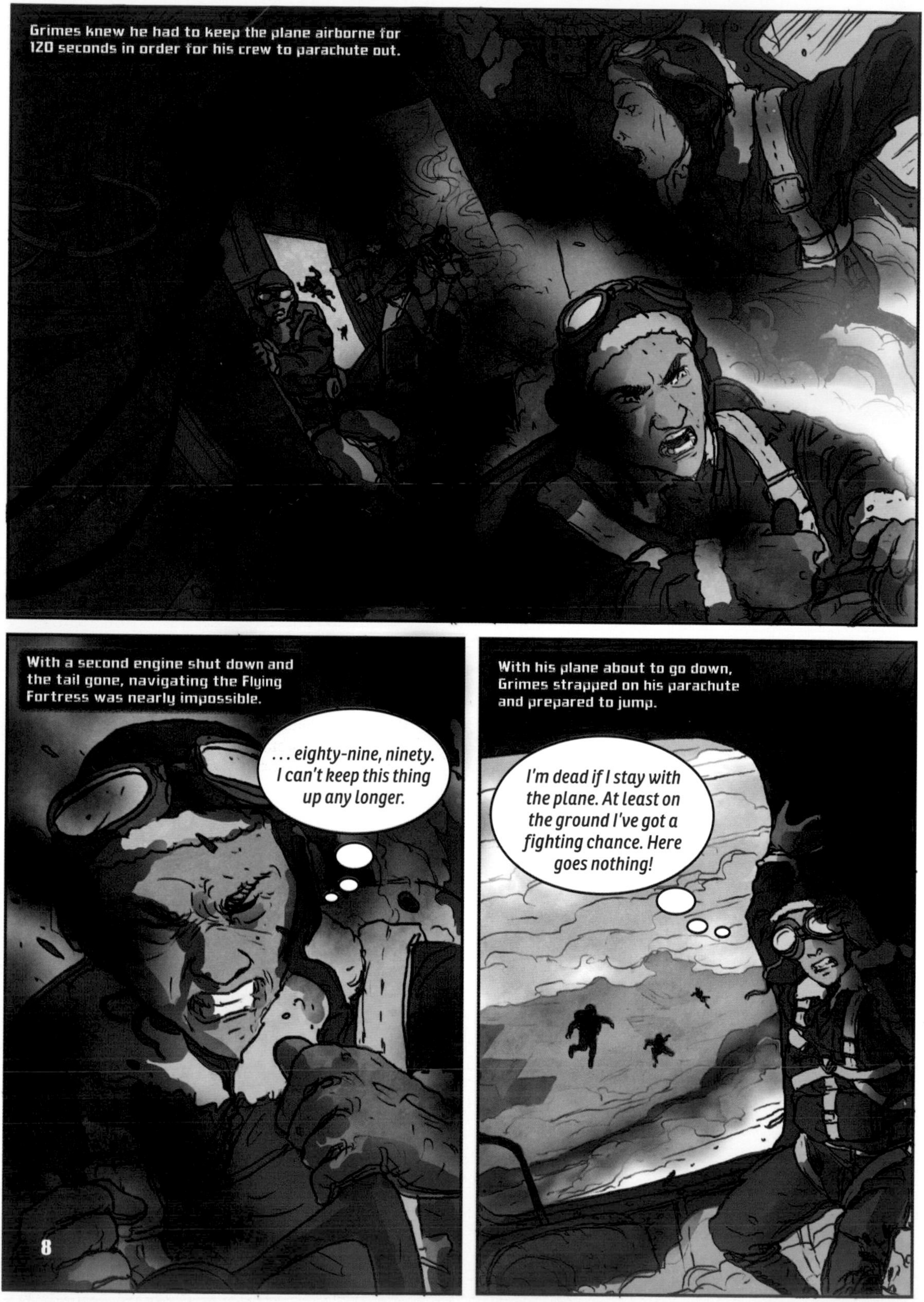
Grimes knew he had to keep the plane airborne for 120 seconds in order for his crew to parachute out.
With a second engine shut down and the tail gone, navigating the Flying Fortress was nearly impossible.
. . . eighty-nine, ninety. I can't keep this thing up any longer.
With his plane about to go down, Grimes strapped on his parachute and prepared to jump.
I'm dead if I stay with the plane. At least on the ground I've got a fighting chance. Here goes nothing!

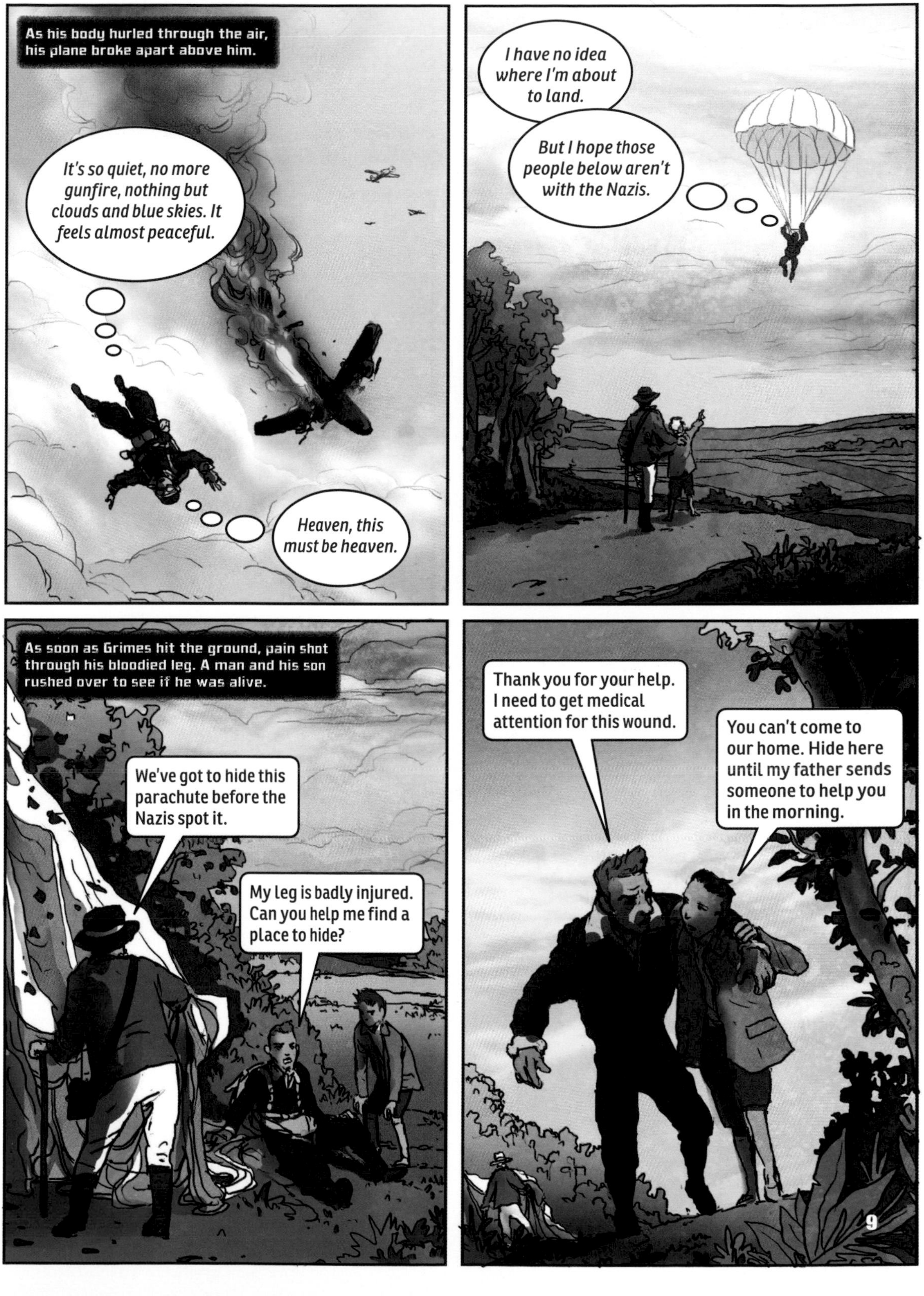
As his body hurled through the air, his plane broke apart above him.
It's so quiet, no more gunfire, nothing but clouds and blue skies. It feels almost peaceful.
Heaven, this must be heaven.
I have no idea where I'm about to land.
But I hope those people below aren't with the Nazis.
As soon as Grimes hit the ground, pain shot through his bloodied leg. A man and his son rushed over to see if he was alive.
We've got to hide this parachute before the Nazis spot it.
My leg is badly injured. Can you help me find a place to hide?
Thank you for your help. I need to get medical attention for this wound.
You can't come to our home. Hide here until my father sends someone to help you in the morning.

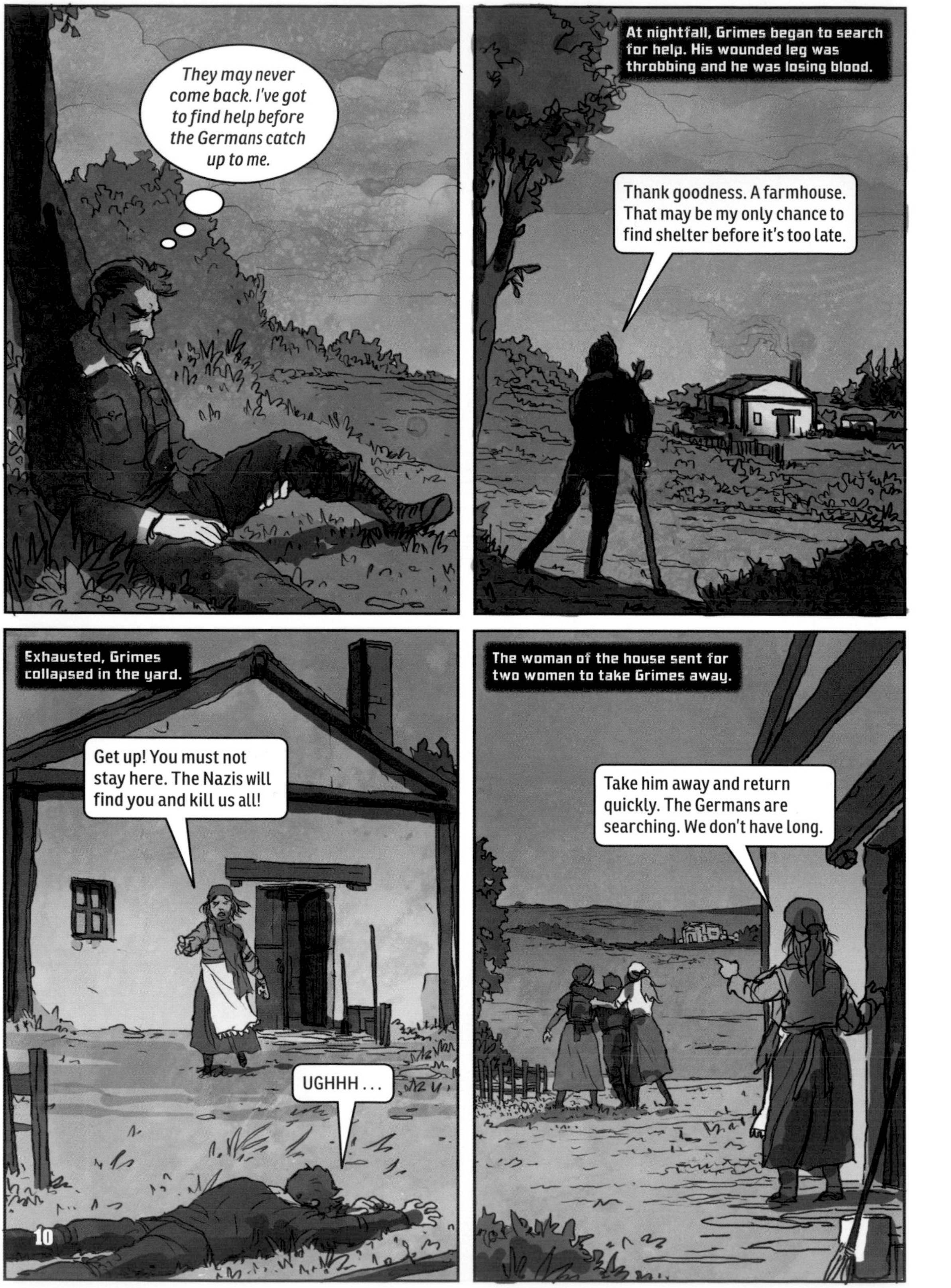
They may never come back. I've got to find help before the Germans catch up to me.
At nightfall, Grimes began to search for help. His wounded leg was throbbing and he was losing blood.
Thank goodness. A farmhouse. That may be my only chance to find shelter before it's too late.
Exhausted, Grimes collapsed in the yard.
Get up! You must not stay here. The Nazis will find you and kill us all!
UGHHH . . .
The woman of the house sent for two women to take Grimes away.
Take him away and return quickly. The Germans are searching. We don't have long.

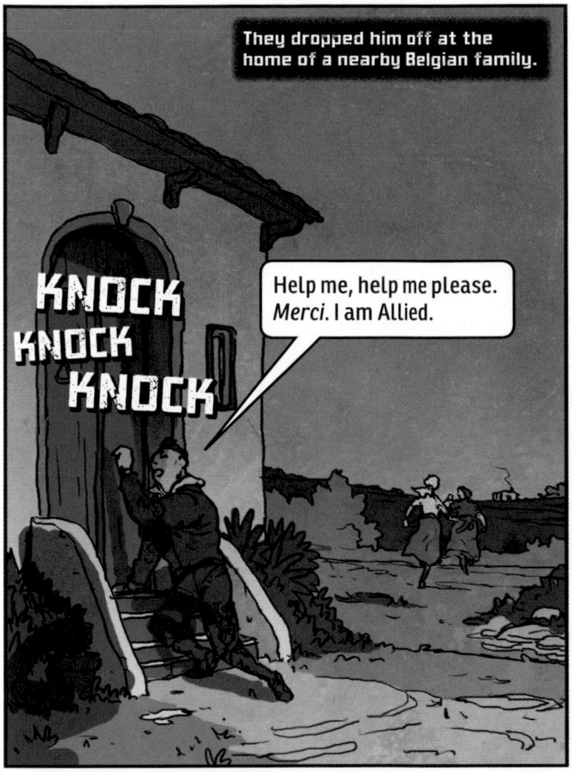
They dropped him off at the home of a nearby Belgian family.
KNOCK KNOCK KNOCK
Help me, help me please. *Merci*. I am Allied.

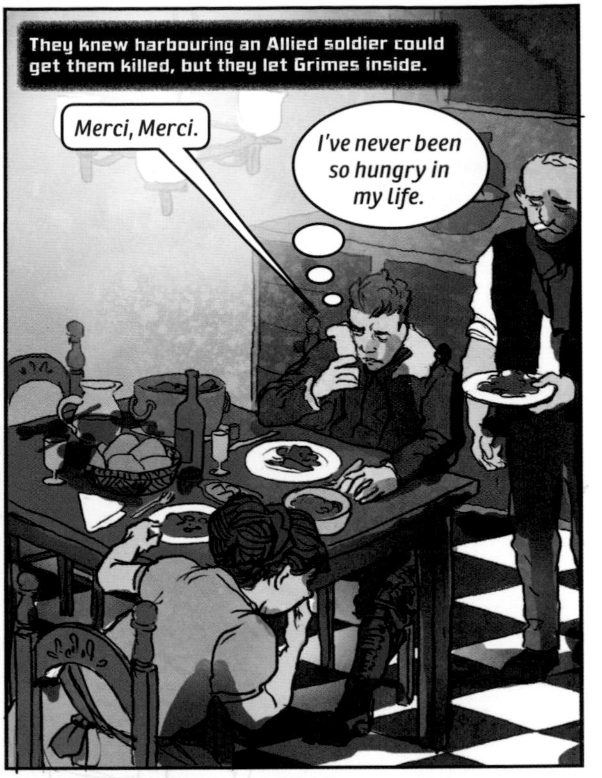
They knew harbouring an Allied soldier could get them killed, but they let Grimes inside.
Merci, Merci.
I've never been so hungry in my life.

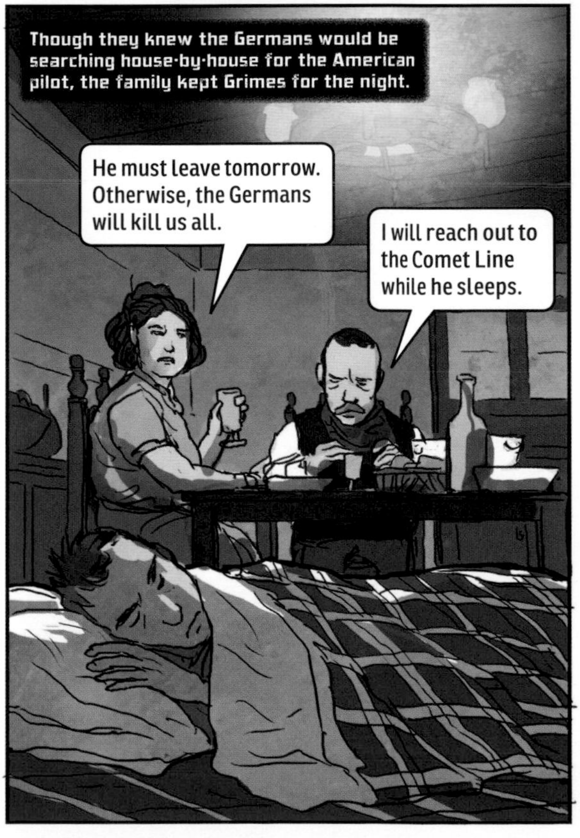
Though they knew the Germans would be searching house-by-house for the American pilot, the family kept Grimes for the night.
He must leave tomorrow. Otherwise, the Germans will kill us all.
I will reach out to the Comet Line while he sleeps.

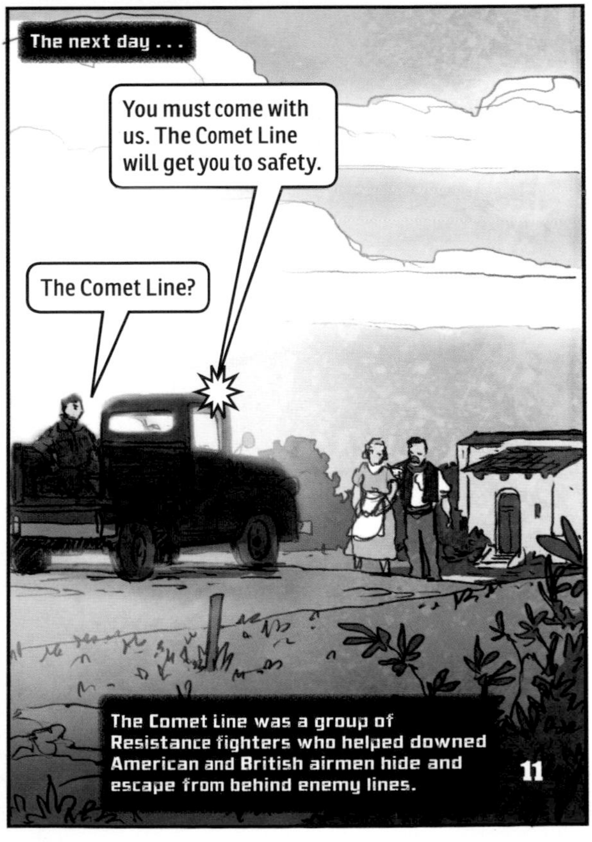
The next day . . .
You must come with us. The Comet Line will get you to safety.
The Comet Line?
The Comet line was a group of Resistance fighters who helped downed American and British airmen hide and escape from behind enemy lines.

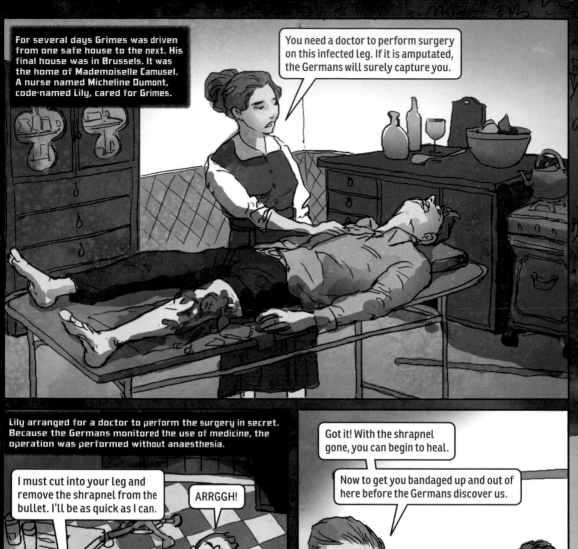

For several days Grimes was driven from one safe house to the next. His final house was in Brussels. It was the home of Mademoiselle Camusel. A nurse named Micheline Dumont, code-named Lily, cared for Grimes.

You need a doctor to perform surgery on this infected leg. If it is amputated, the Germans will surely capture you.

Lily arranged for a doctor to perform the surgery in secret. Because the Germans monitored the use of medicine, the operation was performed without anaesthesia.

I must cut into your leg and remove the shrapnel from the bullet. I'll be as quick as I can.

ARRGGH!

Got it! With the shrapnel gone, you can begin to heal.

Now to get you bandaged up and out of here before the Germans discover us.

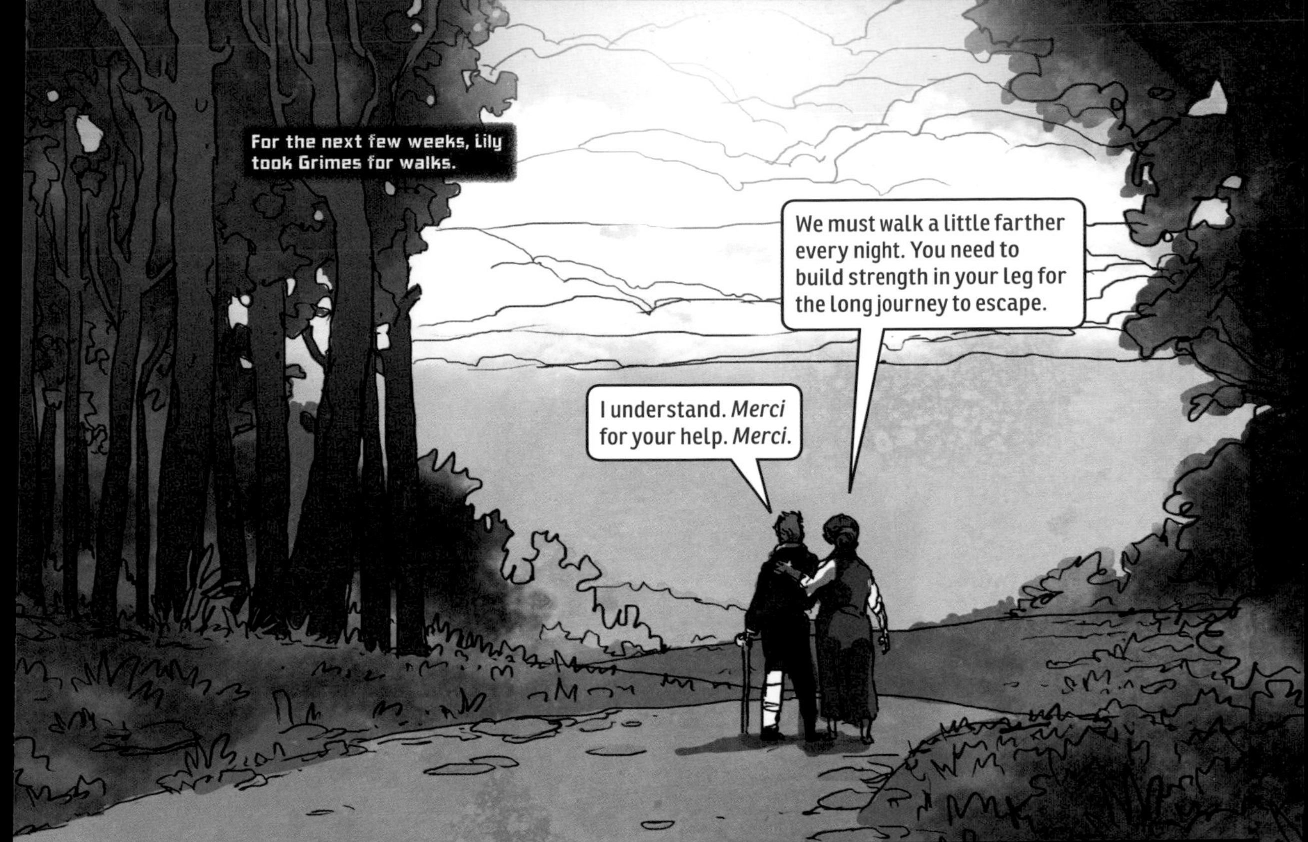
For the next few weeks, Lily took Grimes for walks.
We must walk a little farther every night. You need to build strength in your leg for the long journey to escape.
I understand. *Merci* for your help. *Merci*.

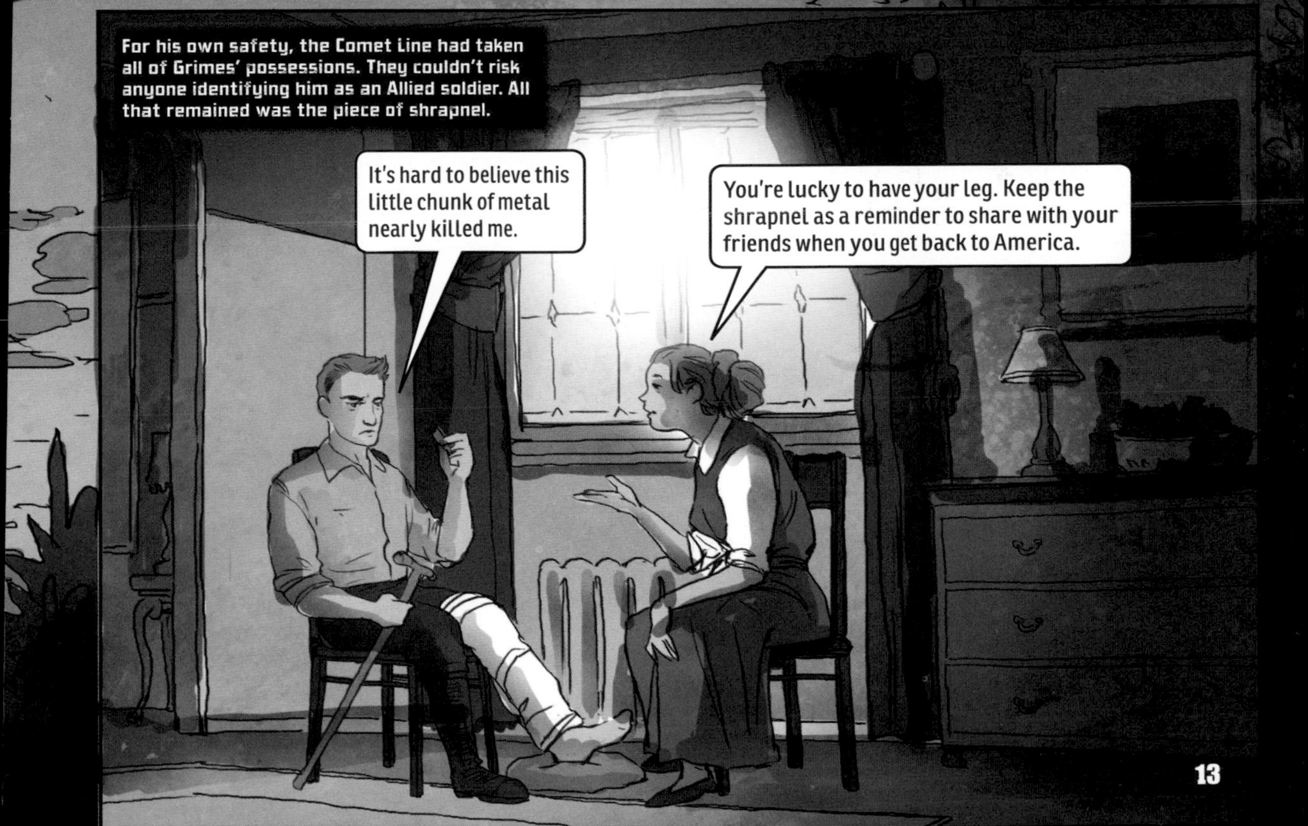
For his own safety, the Comet Line had taken all of Grimes' possessions. They couldn't risk anyone identifying him as an Allied soldier. All that remained was the piece of shrapnel.
It's hard to believe this little chunk of metal nearly killed me.
You're lucky to have your leg. Keep the shrapnel as a reminder to share with your friends when you get back to America.

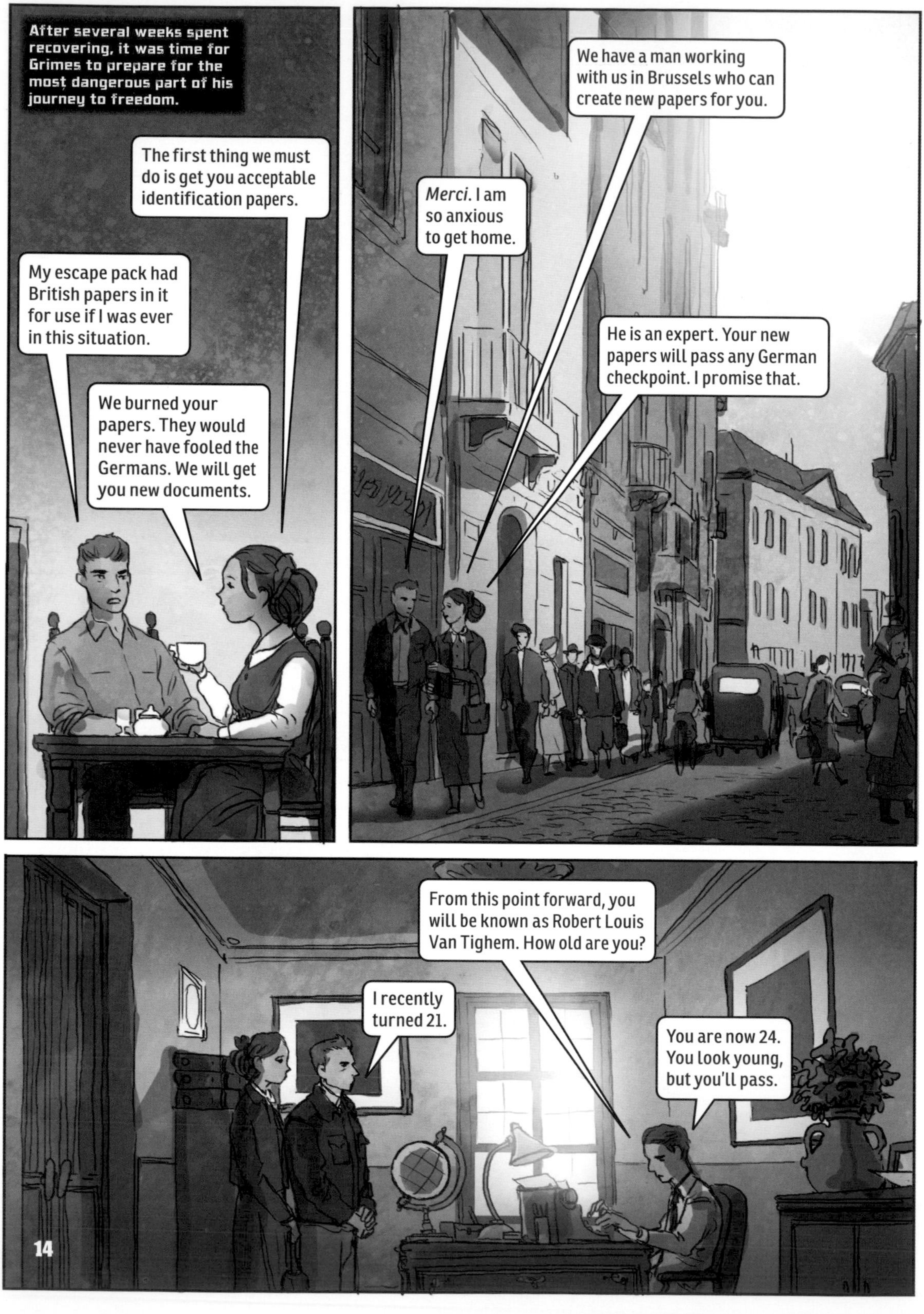
After several weeks spent recovering, it was time for Grimes to prepare for the most dangerous part of his journey to freedom.
The first thing we must do is get you acceptable identification papers.
My escape pack had British papers in it for use if I was ever in this situation.
We burned your papers. They would never have fooled the Germans. We will get you new documents.
We have a man working with us in Brussels who can create new papers for you.
Merci. I am so anxious to get home.
He is an expert. Your new papers will pass any German checkpoint. I promise that.
From this point forward, you will be known as Robert Louis Van Tighem. How old are you?
I recently turned 21.
You are now 24. You look young, but you'll pass.

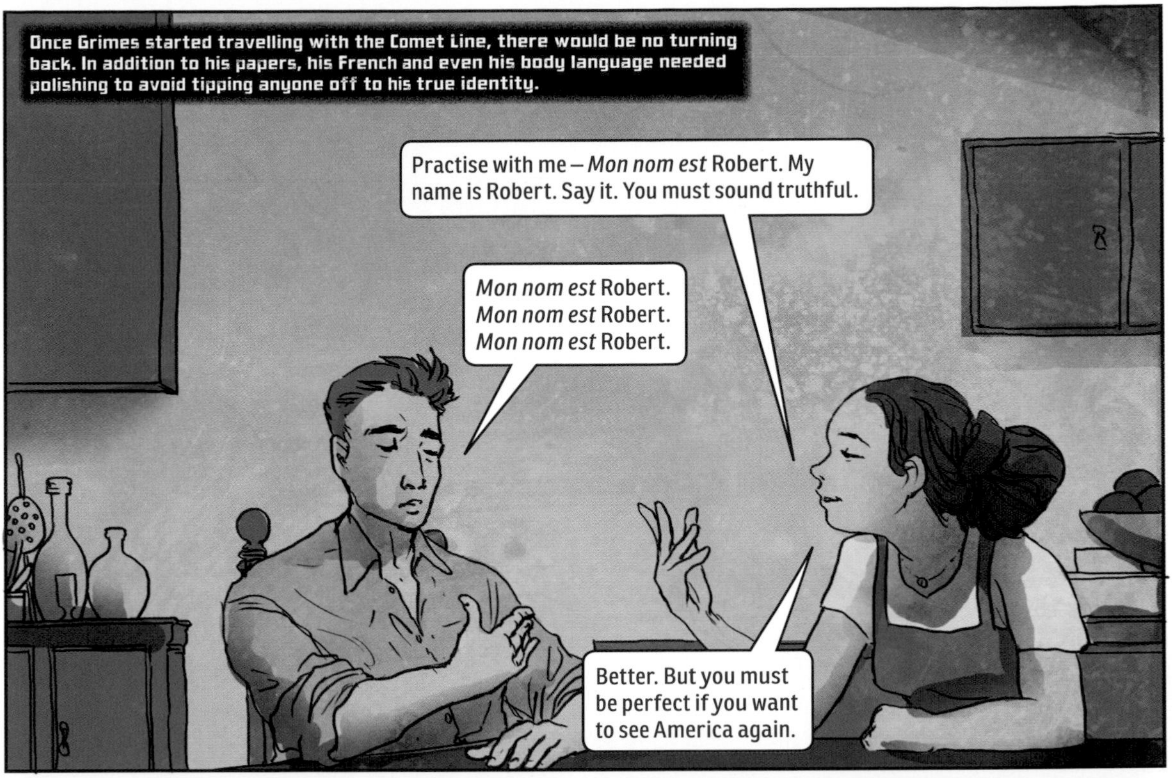
Once Grimes started travelling with the Comet Line, there would be no turning back. In addition to his papers, his French and even his body language needed polishing to avoid tipping anyone off to his true identity.
Practise with me – *Mon nom est* Robert. My name is Robert. Say it. You must sound truthful.
Mon nom est Robert. *Mon nom est* Robert. *Mon nom est* Robert.
Better. But you must be perfect if you want to see America again.

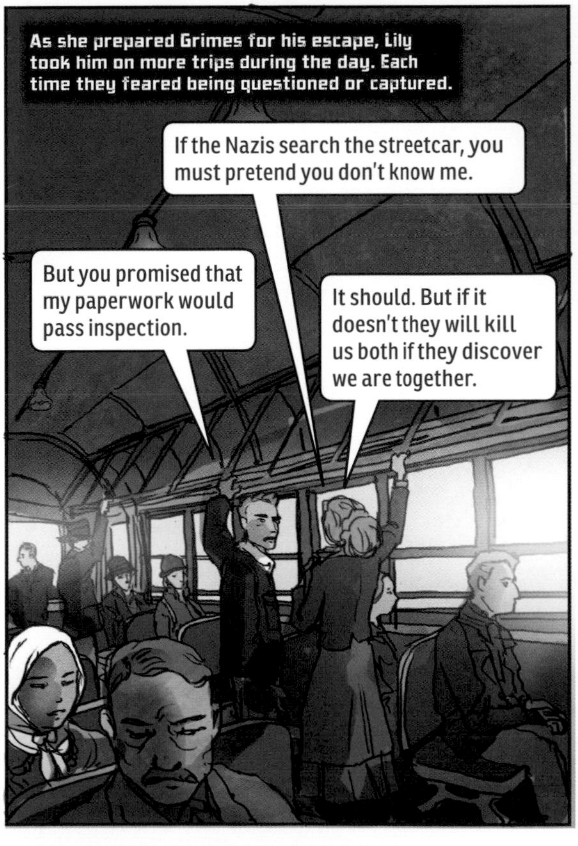
As she prepared Grimes for his escape, Lily took him on more trips during the day. Each time they feared being questioned or captured.
If the Nazis search the streetcar, you must pretend you don't know me.
But you promised that my paperwork would pass inspection.
It should. But if it doesn't they will kill us both if they discover we are together.

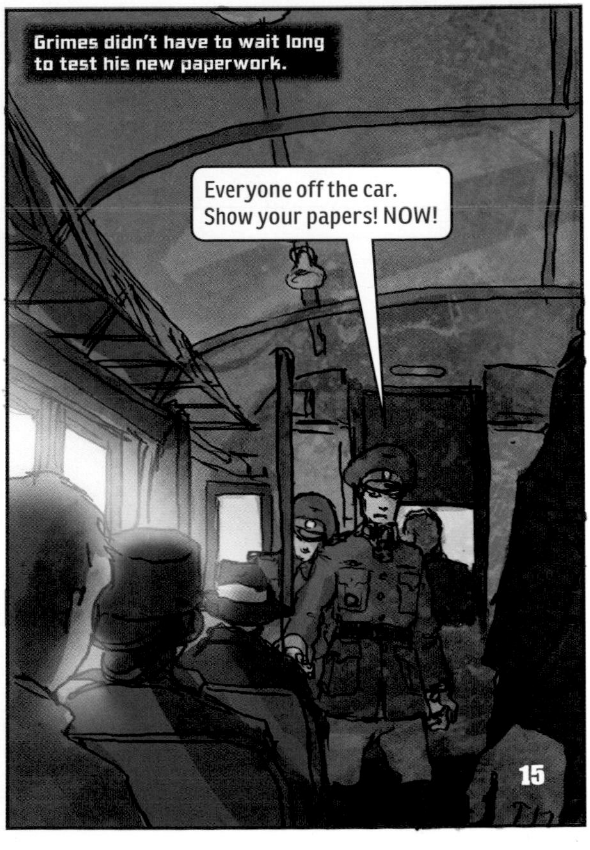
Grimes didn't have to wait long to test his new paperwork.
Everyone off the car. Show your papers! NOW!

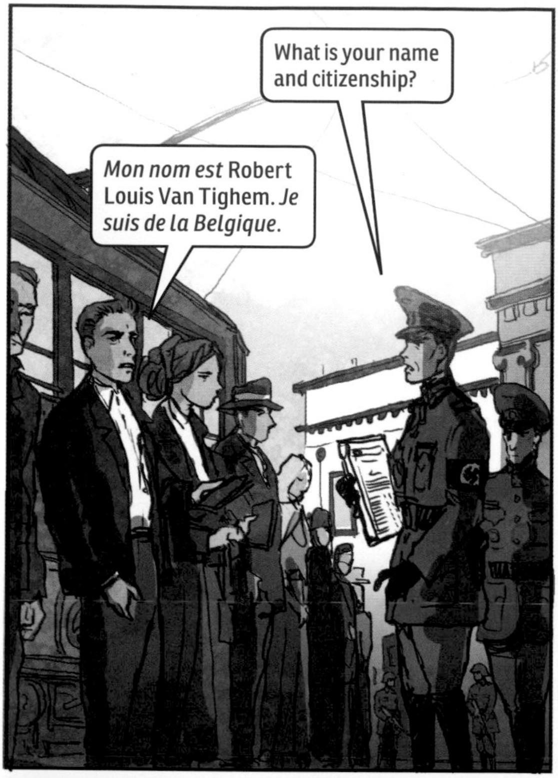
What is your name and citizenship?
Mon nom est Robert Louis Van Tighem. *Je suis de la Belgique*.

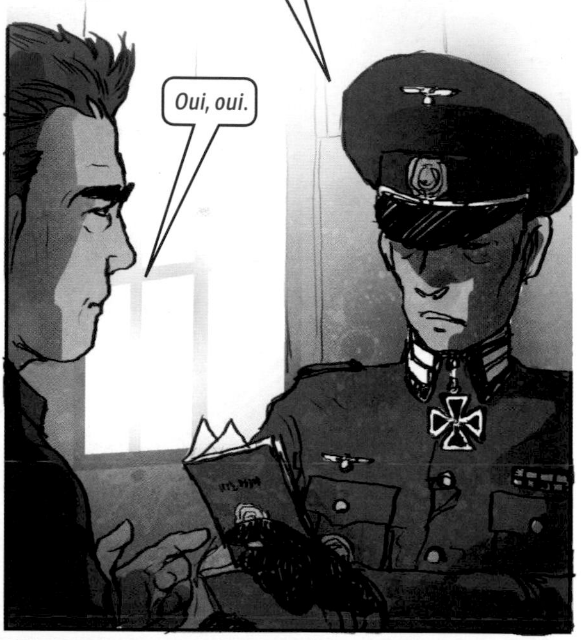
Get back on the streetcar.
Oui, oui.

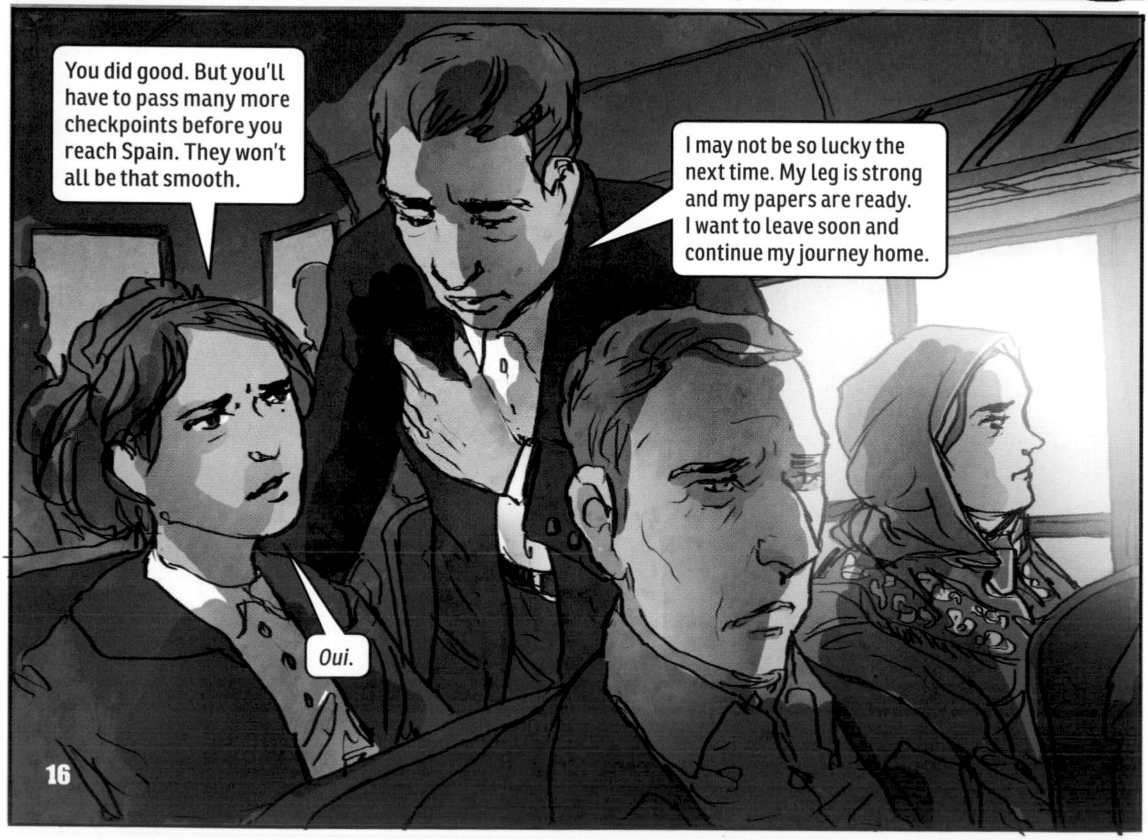
You did good. But you'll have to pass many more checkpoints before you reach Spain. They won't all be that smooth.
Oui.
I may not be so lucky the next time. My leg is strong and my papers are ready. I want to leave soon and continue my journey home.

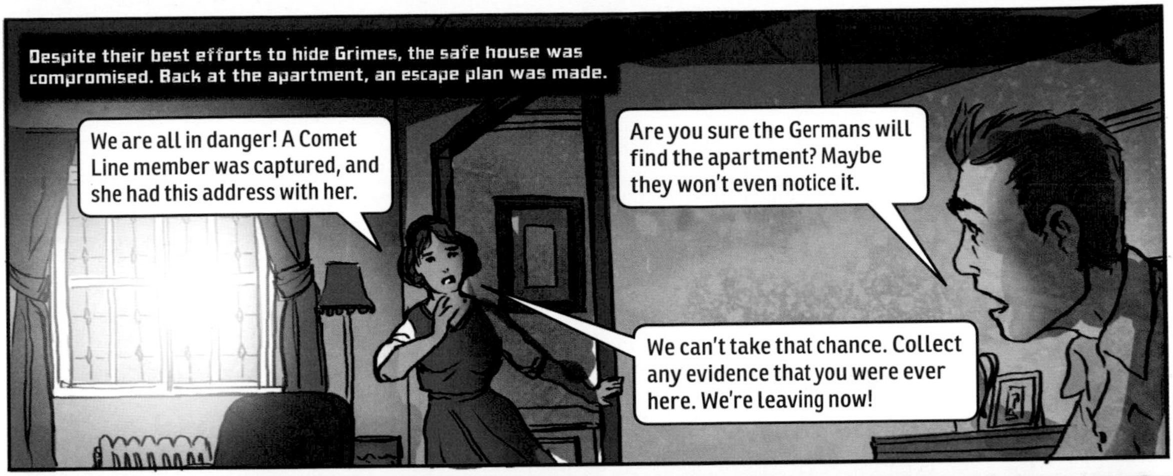
Despite their best efforts to hide Grimes, the safe house was compromised. Back at the apartment, an escape plan was made.
We are all in danger! A Comet Line member was captured, and she had this address with her.
Are you sure the Germans will find the apartment? Maybe they won't even notice it.
We can't take that chance. Collect any evidence that you were ever here. We're leaving now!

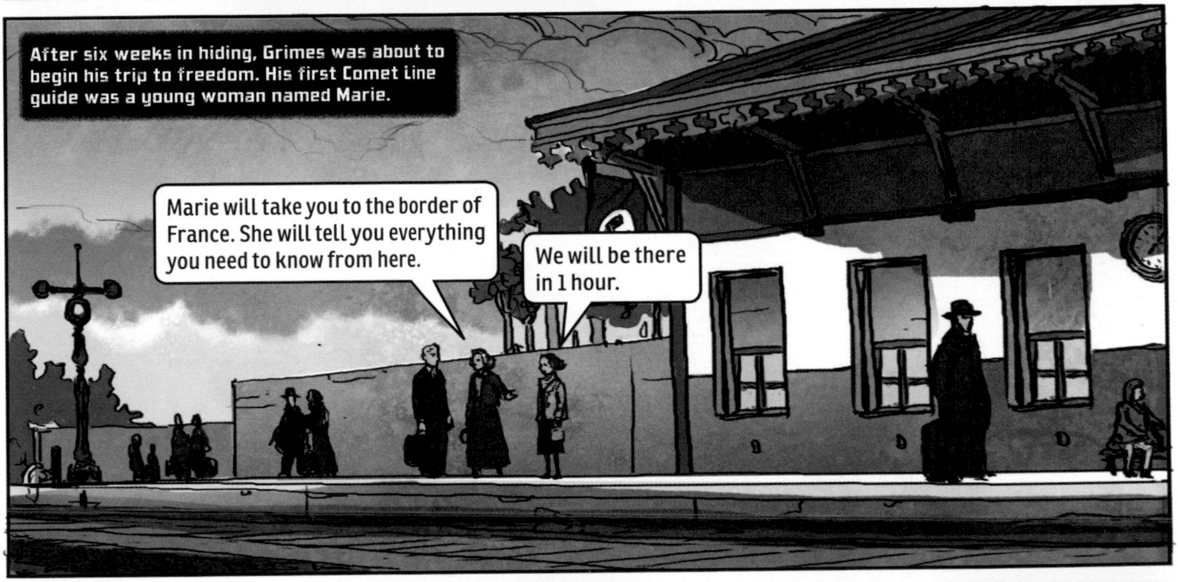
After six weeks in hiding, Grimes was about to begin his trip to freedom. His first Comet Line guide was a young woman named Marie.
Marie will take you to the border of France. She will tell you everything you need to know from here.
We will be there in 1 hour.

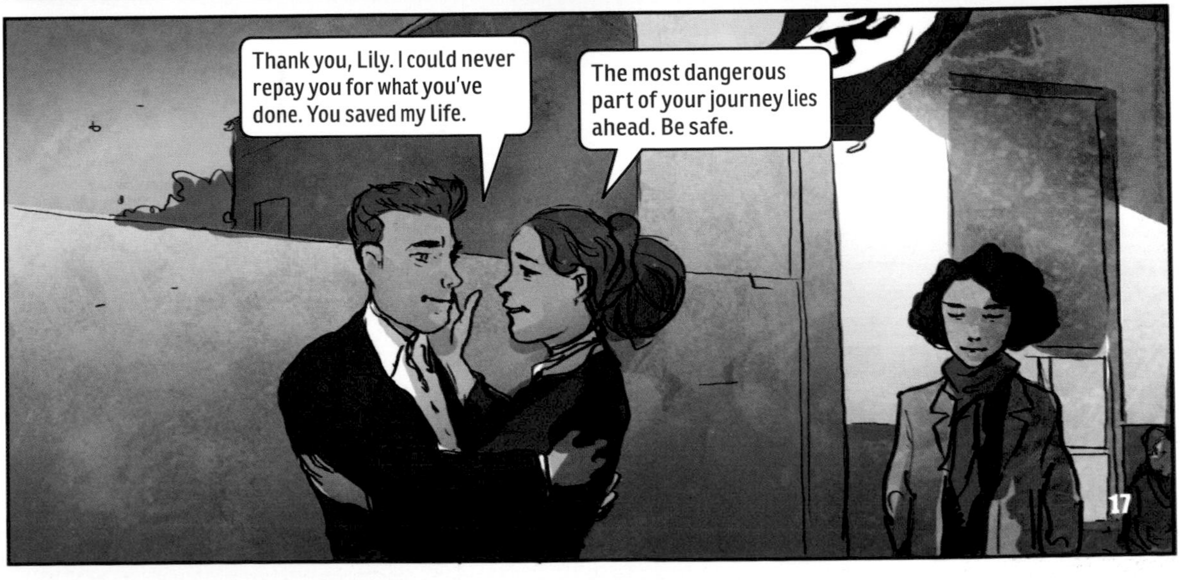
Thank you, Lily. I could never repay you for what you've done. You saved my life.
The most dangerous part of your journey lies ahead. Be safe.

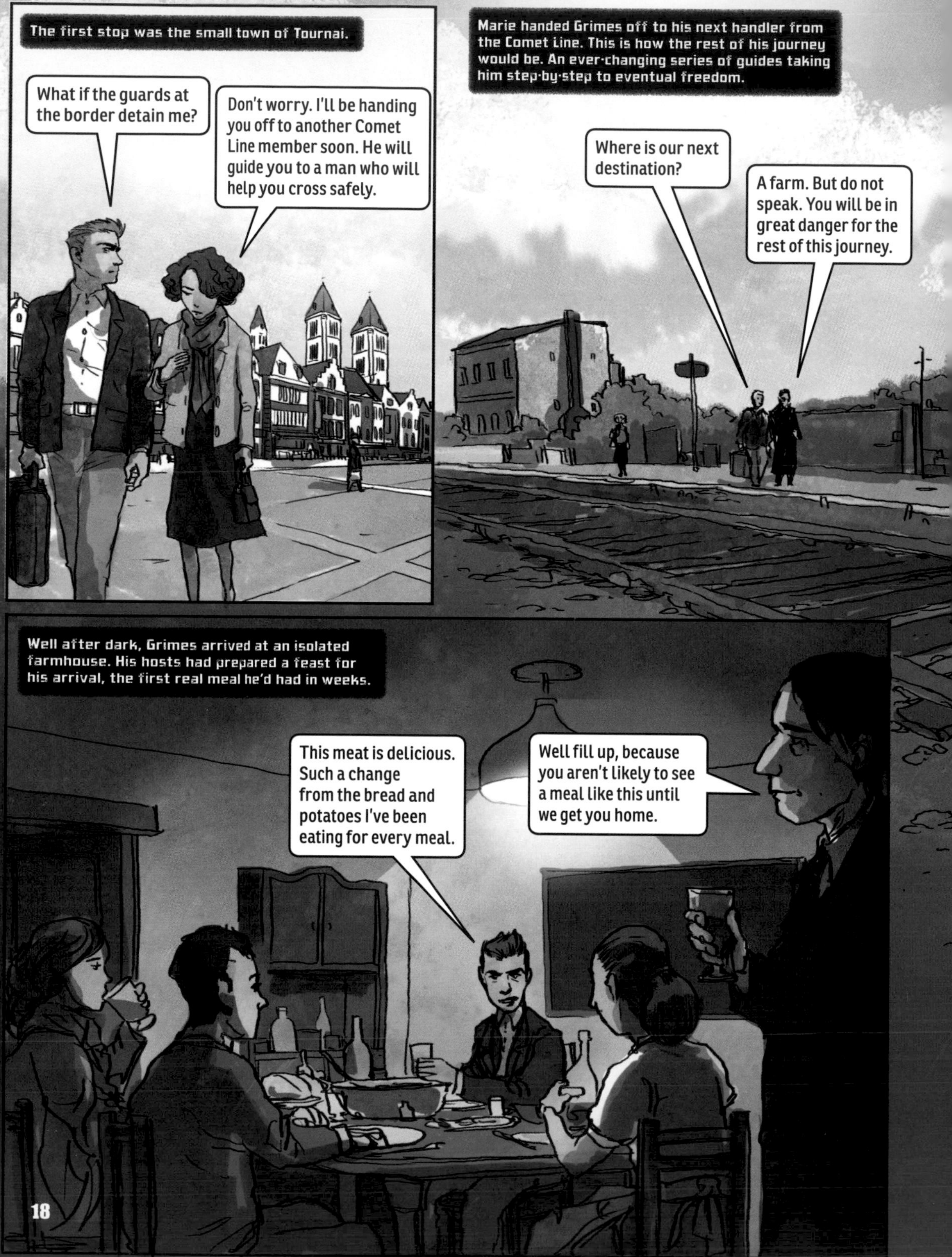
The first stop was the small town of Tournai.
What if the guards at the border detain me?
Don't worry. I'll be handing you off to another Comet Line member soon. He will guide you to a man who will help you cross safely.
Marie handed Grimes off to his next handler from the Comet Line. This is how the rest of his journey would be. An ever-changing series of guides taking him step-by-step to eventual freedom.
Where is our next destination?
A farm. But do not speak. You will be in great danger for the rest of this journey.
Well after dark, Grimes arrived at an isolated farmhouse. His hosts had prepared a feast for his arrival, the first real meal he'd had in weeks.
This meat is delicious. Such a change from the bread and potatoes I've been eating for every meal.
Well fill up, because you aren't likely to see a meal like this until we get you home.

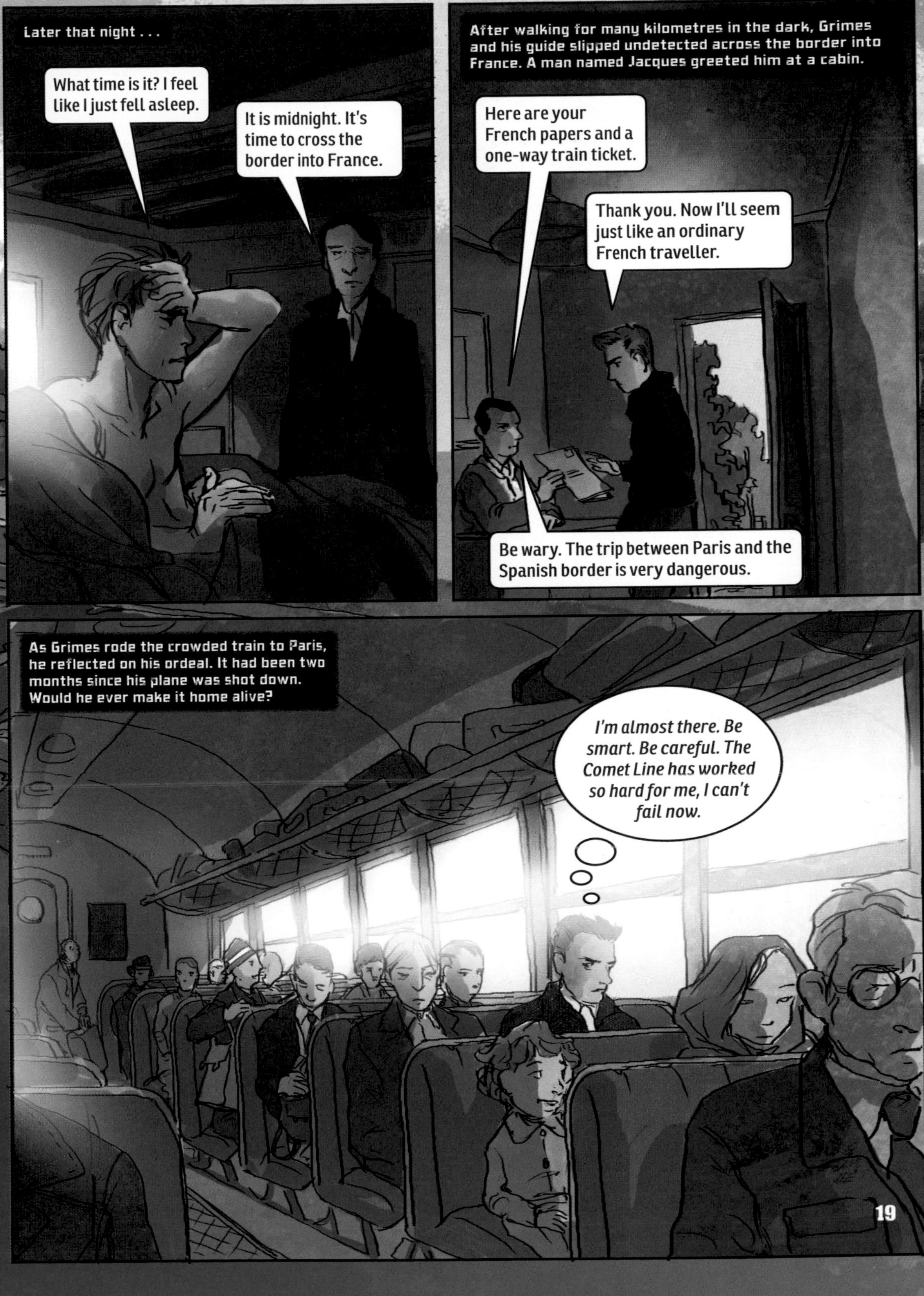
Later that night . . .
What time is it? I feel like I just fell asleep.
It is midnight. It's time to cross the border into France.
After walking for many kilometres in the dark, Grimes and his guide slipped undetected across the border into France. A man named Jacques greeted him at a cabin.
Here are your French papers and a one-way train ticket.
Thank you. Now I'll seem just like an ordinary French traveller.
Be wary. The trip between Paris and the Spanish border is very dangerous.
As Grimes rode the crowded train to Paris, he reflected on his ordeal. It had been two months since his plane was shot down. Would he ever make it home alive?
I'm almost there. Be smart. Be careful. The Comet Line has worked so hard for me, I can't fail now.

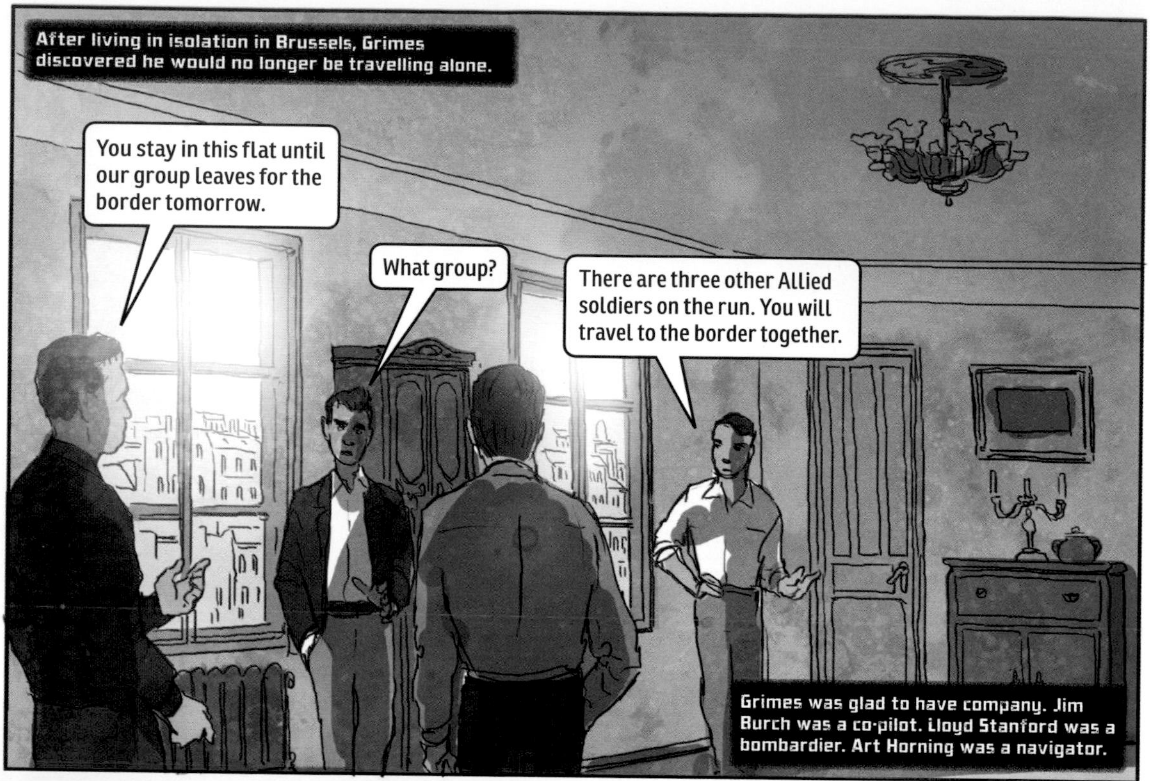
After living in isolation in Brussels, Grimes discovered he would no longer be travelling alone.
You stay in this flat until our group leaves for the border tomorrow.
What group?
There are three other Allied soldiers on the run. You will travel to the border together.
Grimes was glad to have company. Jim Burch was a co-pilot. Lloyd Stanford was a bombardier. Art Horning was a navigator.

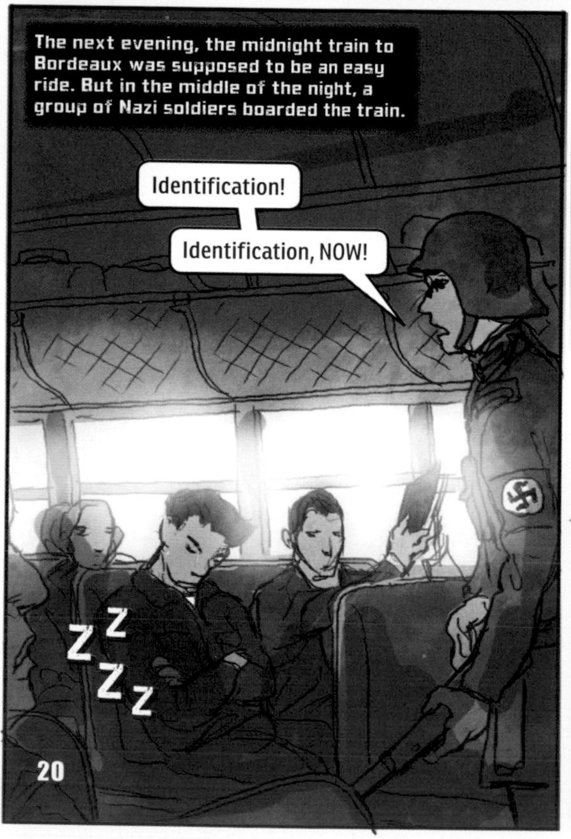
The next evening, the midnight train to Bordeaux was supposed to be an easy ride. But in the middle of the night, a group of Nazi soldiers boarded the train.
Identification!
Identification, NOW!
Z Z Z Z

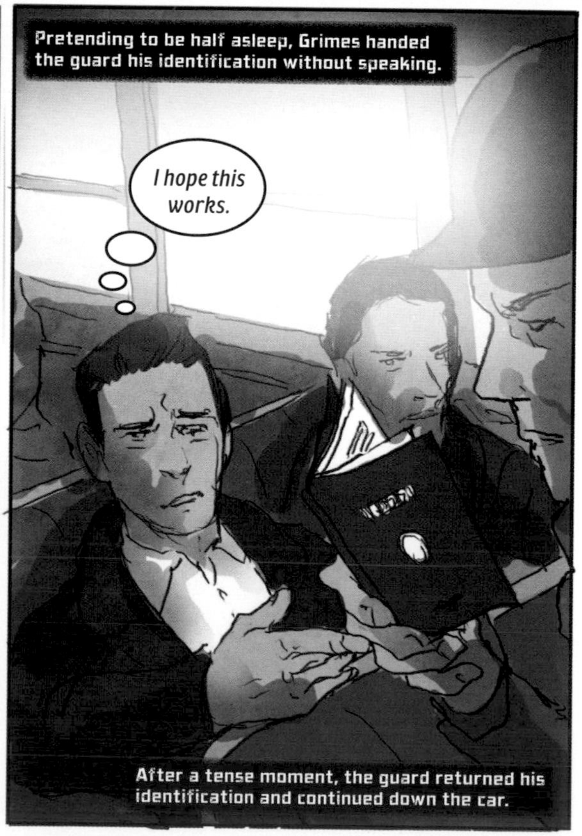
Pretending to be half asleep, Grimes handed the guard his identification without speaking.
I hope this works.
After a tense moment, the guard returned his identification and continued down the car.

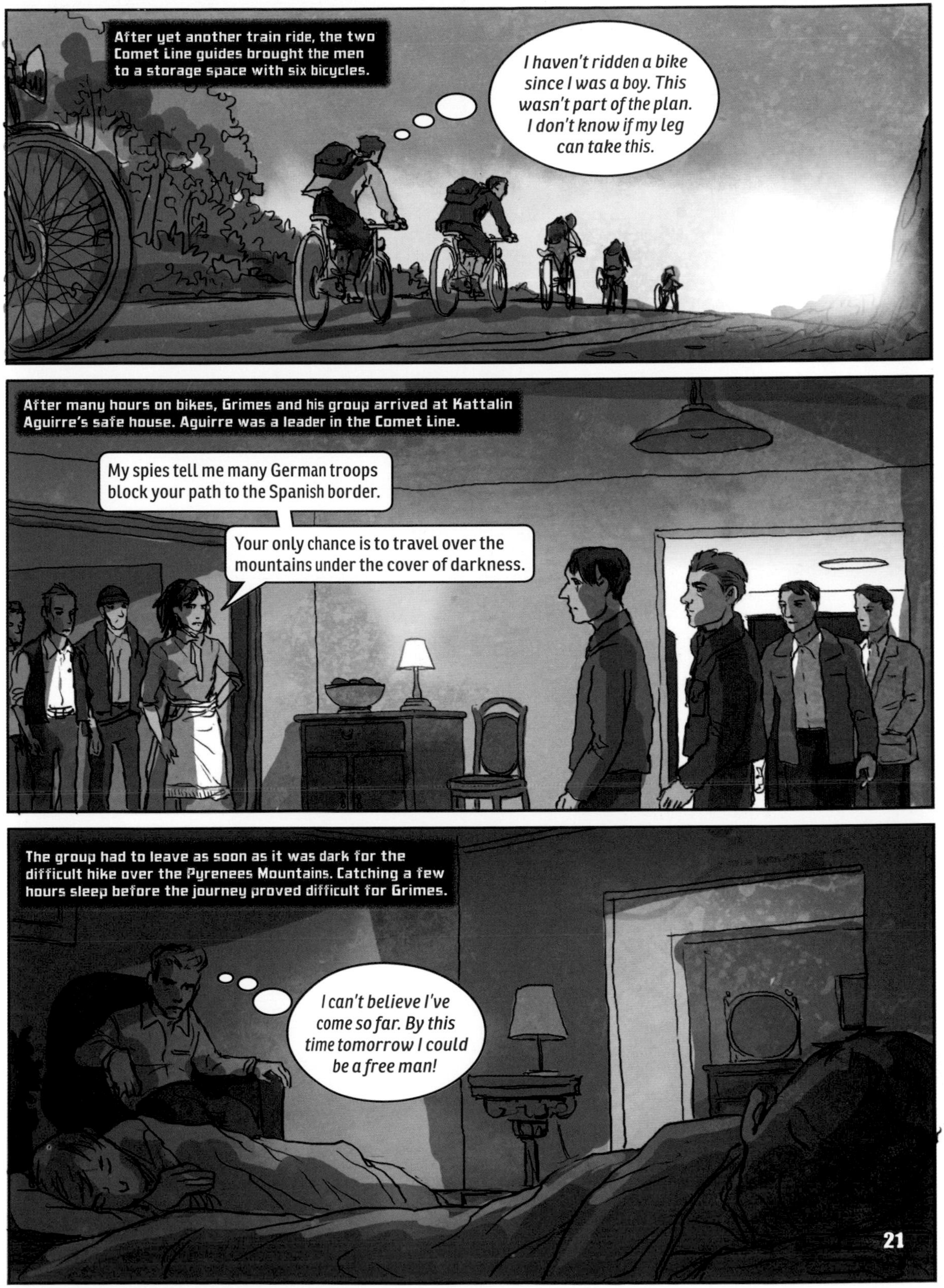
After yet another train ride, the two Comet Line guides brought the men to a storage space with six bicycles.
I haven't ridden a bike since I was a boy. This wasn't part of the plan. I don't know if my leg can take this.
After many hours on bikes, Grimes and his group arrived at Kattalin Aguirre's safe house. Aguirre was a leader in the Comet Line.
My spies tell me many German troops block your path to the Spanish border.
Your only chance is to travel over the mountains under the cover of darkness.
The group had to leave as soon as it was dark for the difficult hike over the Pyrenees Mountains. Catching a few hours sleep before the journey proved difficult for Grimes.
I can't believe I've come so far. By this time tomorrow I could be a free man!

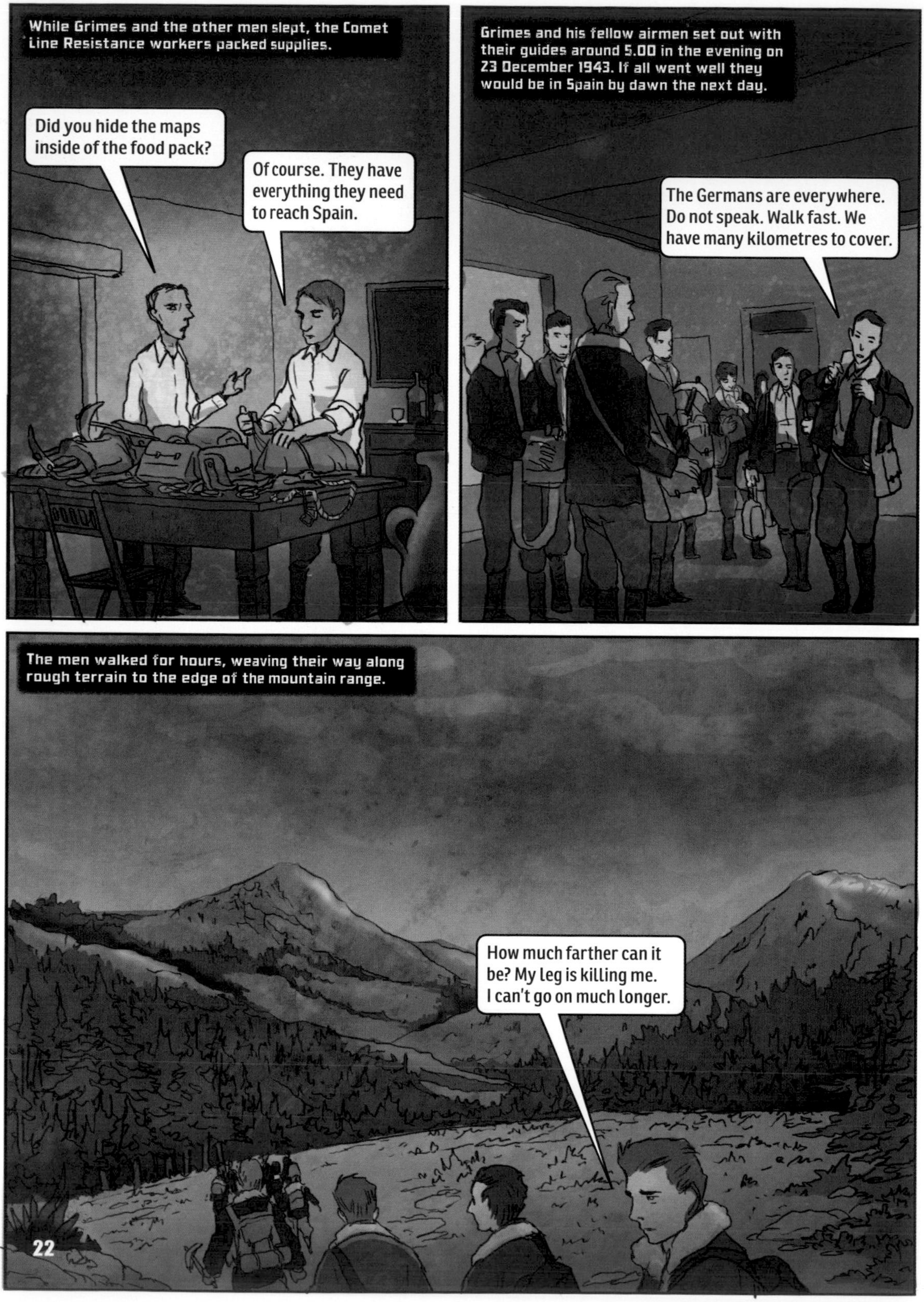
While Grimes and the other men slept, the Comet Line Resistance workers packed supplies.
Did you hide the maps inside of the food pack?
Of course. They have everything they need to reach Spain.
Grimes and his fellow airmen set out with their guides around 5.00 in the evening on 23 December 1943. If all went well they would be in Spain by dawn the next day.
The Germans are everywhere. Do not speak. Walk fast. We have many kilometres to cover.
The men walked for hours, weaving their way along rough terrain to the edge of the mountain range.
How much farther can it be? My leg is killing me. I can't go on much longer.

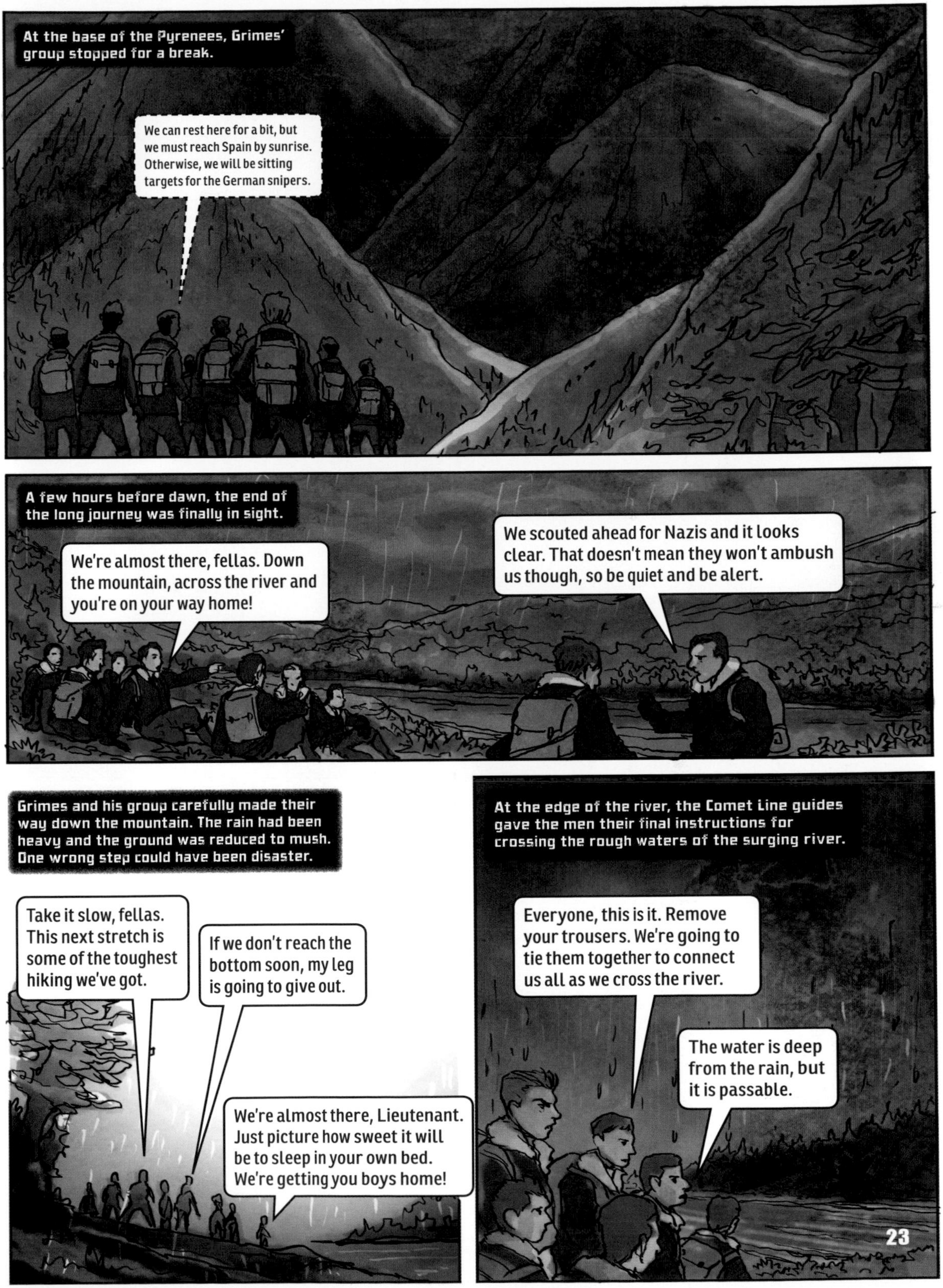
At the base of the Pyrenees, Grimes' group stopped for a break.
We can rest here for a bit, but we must reach Spain by sunrise. Otherwise, we will be sitting targets for the German snipers.
A few hours before dawn, the end of the long journey was finally in sight.
We're almost there, fellas. Down the mountain, across the river and you're on your way home!
We scouted ahead for Nazis and it looks clear. That doesn't mean they won't ambush us though, so be quiet and be alert.
Grimes and his group carefully made their way down the mountain. The rain had been heavy and the ground was reduced to mush. One wrong step could have been disaster.
Take it slow, fellas. This next stretch is some of the toughest hiking we've got.
If we don't reach the bottom soon, my leg is going to give out.
We're almost there, Lieutenant. Just picture how sweet it will be to sleep in your own bed. We're getting you boys home!
At the edge of the river, the Comet Line guides gave the men their final instructions for crossing the rough waters of the surging river.
Everyone, this is it. Remove your trousers. We're going to tie them together to connect us all as we cross the river.
The water is deep from the rain, but it is passable.

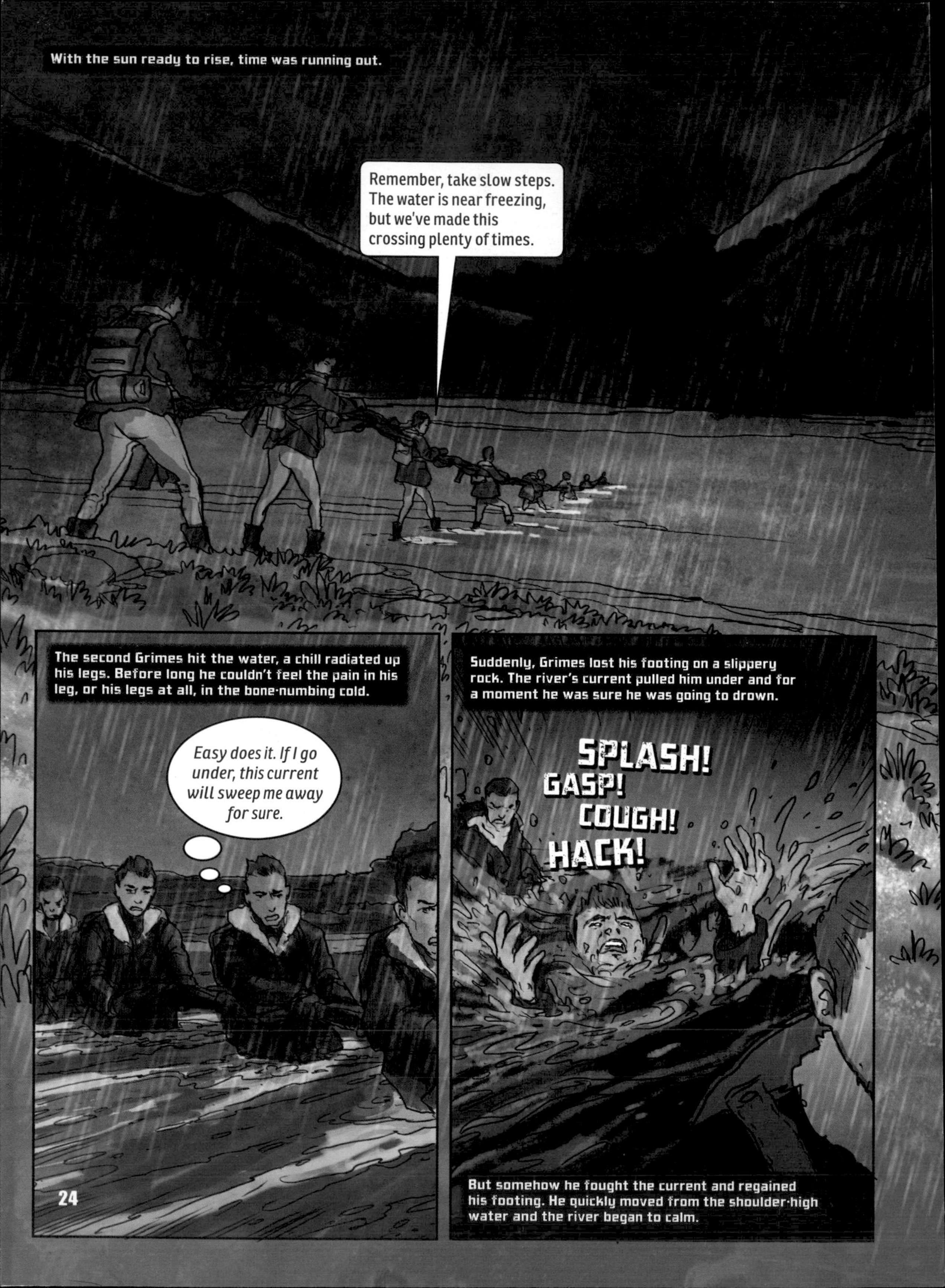
With the sun ready to rise, time was running out.
Remember, take slow steps. The water is near freezing, but we've made this crossing plenty of times.
The second Grimes hit the water, a chill radiated up his legs. Before long he couldn't feel the pain in his leg, or his legs at all, in the bone-numbing cold.
Easy does it. If I go under, this current will sweep me away for sure.
Suddenly, Grimes lost his footing on a slippery rock. The river's current pulled him under and for a moment he was sure he was going to drown.
SPLASH!
GASP!
COUGH!
HACK!
But somehow he fought the current and regained his footing. He quickly moved from the shoulder-high water and the river began to calm.

Suddenly, gunshots rang out. Grimes looked back for his fellow airmen. Stanford and Horning were pulling themselves out of the water. But Burch had been swept away by the mighty current.

...Grimes could hear the soldiers above him, but he couldn't figure out why they were shooting at his group.

On the ground! On the ground! Take cover.

POP
POP
POP

Why are they shooting at us from the Spanish bank? Isn't Spain a friendly country?

We can't die now! We made it to Spain. We're supposed to be FREE!

The Spanish soldiers surrounded the three Americans and Daniel Mouton, a Belgian soldier who survived the trek across the water. They held the men at gunpoint.

Who are you? Why are you here?

We are Allied soldiers. We are not the enemy!

Our planes were shot down. We're just trying to get home!

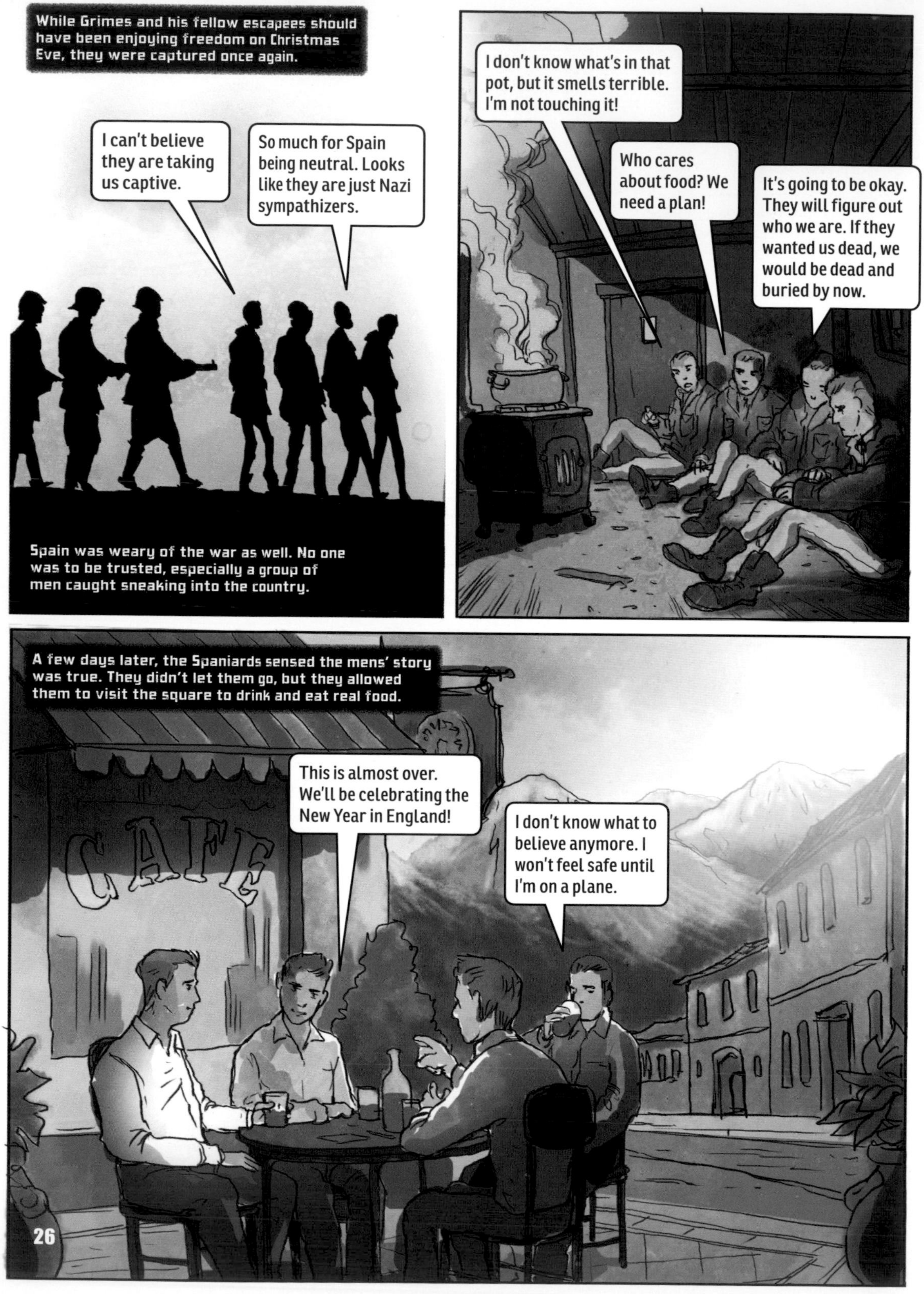
While Grimes and his fellow escapees should have been enjoying freedom on Christmas Eve, they were captured once again.
I can't believe they are taking us captive.
So much for Spain being neutral. Looks like they are just Nazi sympathizers.
Spain was weary of the war as well. No one was to be trusted, especially a group of men caught sneaking into the country.
I don't know what's in that pot, but it smells terrible. I'm not touching it!
Who cares about food? We need a plan!
It's going to be okay. They will figure out who we are. If they wanted us dead, we would be dead and buried by now.
A few days later, the Spaniards sensed the mens' story was true. They didn't let them go, but they allowed them to visit the square to drink and eat real food.
CAFE
This is almost over. We'll be celebrating the New Year in England!
I don't know what to believe anymore. I won't feel safe until I'm on a plane.

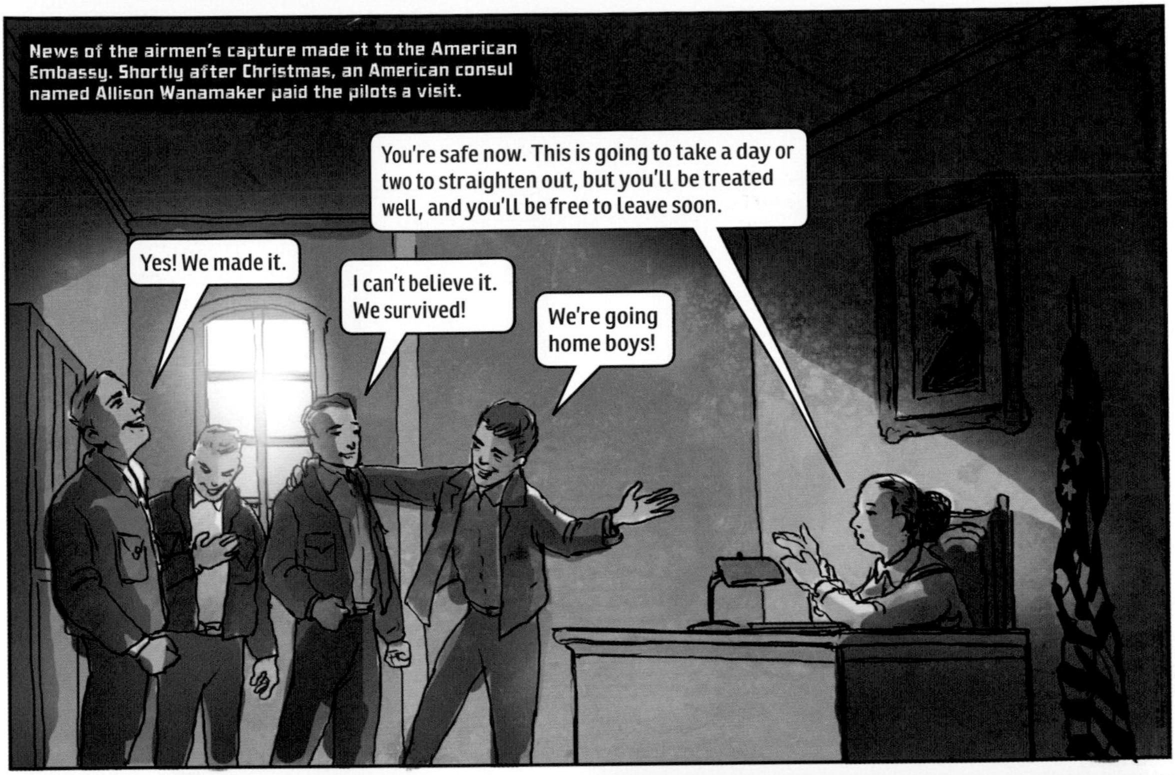
News of the airmen's capture made it to the American Embassy. Shortly after Christmas, an American consul named Allison Wanamaker paid the pilots a visit.
Yes! We made it.
I can't believe it. We survived!
We're going home boys!
You're safe now. This is going to take a day or two to straighten out, but you'll be treated well, and you'll be free to leave soon.

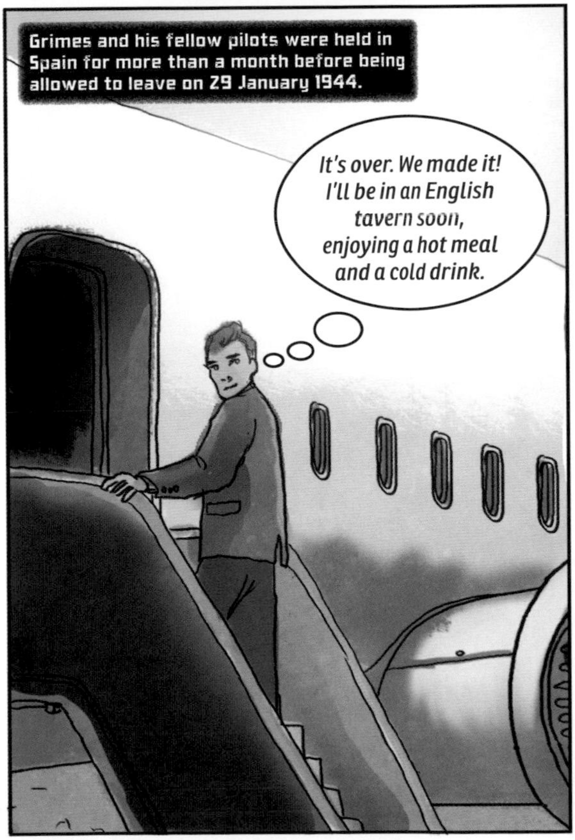
Grimes and his fellow pilots were held in Spain for more than a month before being allowed to leave on 29 January 1944.
It's over. We made it! I'll be in an English tavern soon, enjoying a hot meal and a cold drink.

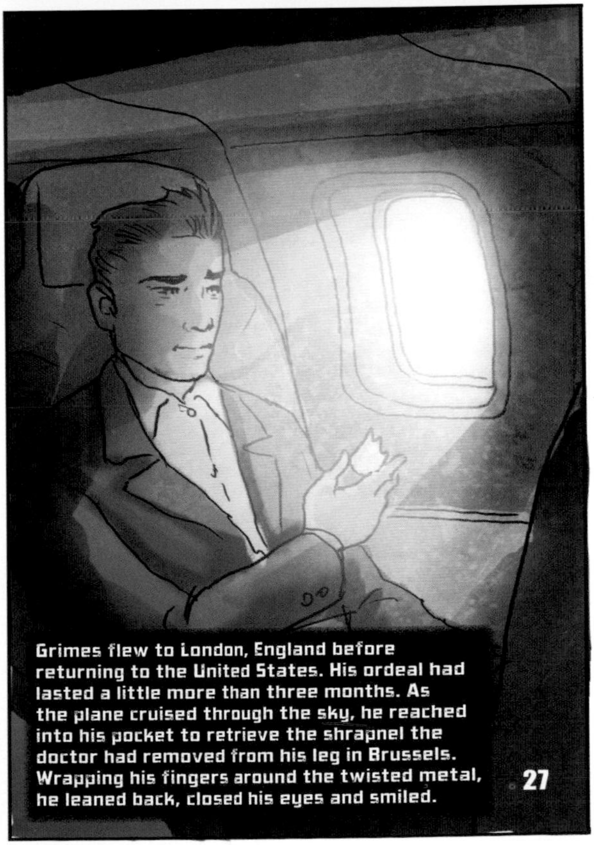
Grimes flew to London, England before returning to the United States. His ordeal had lasted a little more than three months. As the plane cruised through the sky, he reached into his pocket to retrieve the shrapnel the doctor had removed from his leg in Brussels. Wrapping his fingers around the twisted metal, he leaned back, closed his eyes and smiled.

LIFE AFTER THE WAR

Lieutenant Grimes was just 20 years old when he was shot down over Belgium. After gaining his freedom, he returned to the air and flew many more missions in Europe. When the war ended, he remained in the Army and rose to the rank of Colonel. After he retired as a pilot, Grimes joined the staff of the Pentagon. He remained there until his retirement from the military in 1972.

Grimes rarely spoke of his ordeal after the war. His mission, crash and daring escape were all marked Top Secret Classified by the United States government. But that may not have been the only reason why he didn't discuss what happened. He had also lost four men on the B-17 bombing mission. As the pilot, he felt personally responsible for their deaths.

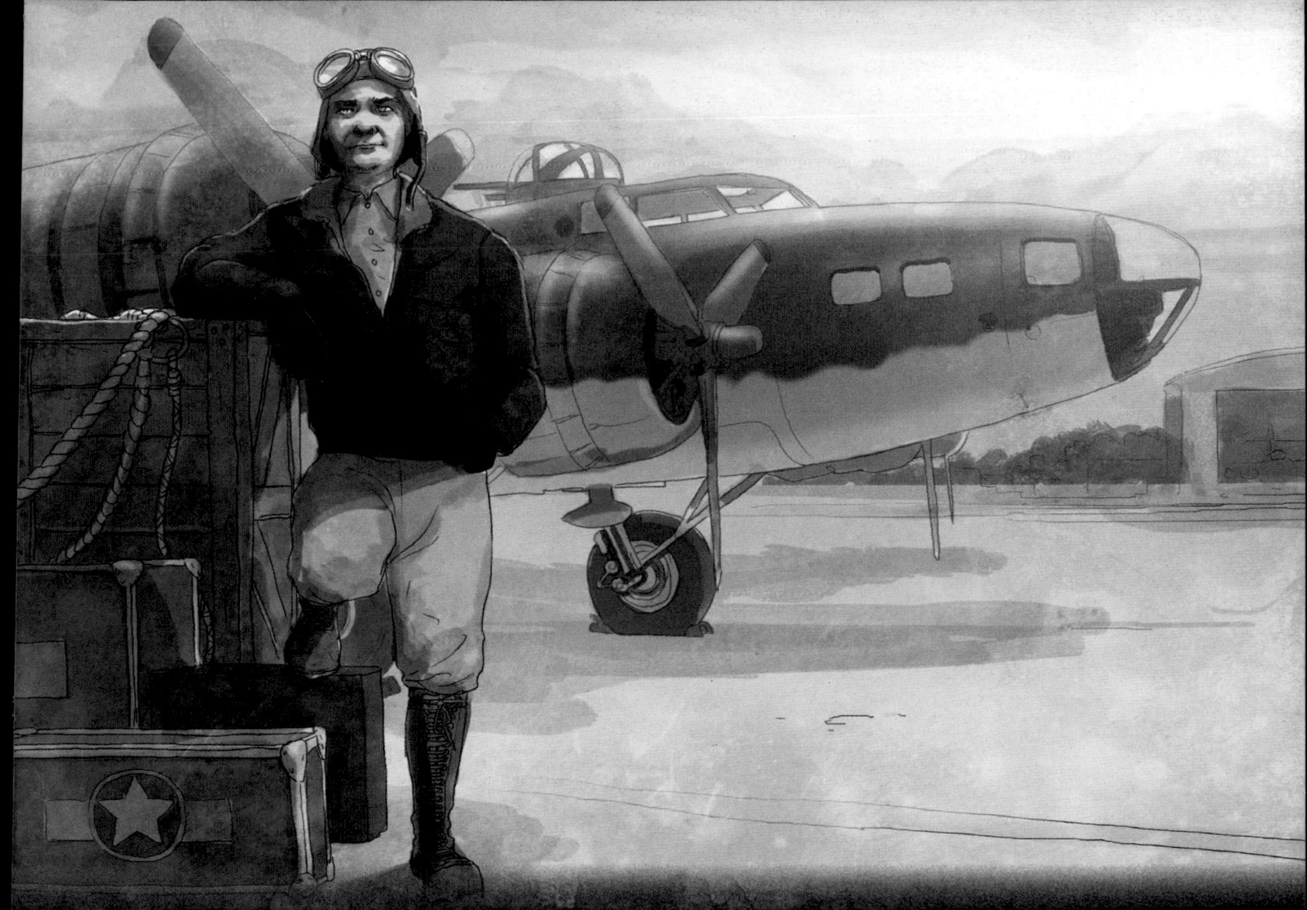

In addition to his military service, Grimes and his wife, Mary Helen, raised three daughters. He also enjoyed a second career as a school administrator in Virginia, USA. Only in the final years of his life did he open up about his experience. While being interviewed by a *Washington Post* reporter in 2004, he described his feelings more than 60 years after being shot down: "You never stop thinking about it. In my mind, I'm back in the cockpit, left seat, looking at the controls, and I'm dodging and diving around the Nazi fighters, trying to make it to a cloud bank. And I look for every option, but I never come up with anything to save us."

Colonel Robert Z. Grimes fought to save his crew in their crippled plane, escaped capture by the Nazis and served honourably for 30 years in the military. He was awarded the Legion of Merit and the Air Medal in addition to a Purple Heart. He passed away in 2010 at the age of 87.

GLOSSARY

ambush surprise attack

anaesthesia gas or injection that prevents pain during treatments and operations

classified top secret

detain hold prisoner

embassy building where representatives from another country work

formation group of aeroplanes flying together in a pattern

harbour shelter and protect someone

isolated all alone

navigator someone who plans and directs the route of a trip

neutral not taking sides

Resistance secret group of fighters that worked against the Nazis in occupied countries of Europe during World War II

safe house place where spies or other secret agents can go for help and protection

shrapnel pieces that have broken off from an explosive shell

squadron official military unit

sympathizer person who supports a group or a cause

COMPREHENSION QUESTIONS

1. Why did Grimes keep the piece of shrapnel from his injured leg? What did it mean to him? How do you know?

2. The portion of this book told in graphic novel format uses both narrative and dialogue. Why does the author use both? How does the use of both types of text help you better understand the story?

3. Assume the identity of a Resistance fighter working for the Comet Line during World War II. Write a diary entry telling your experiences from your point of view. Describe the types of things you would do to help an Allied soldier escape to freedom.

FIND OUT MORE

Great Escapes (War Stories), Charlotte Guillain (Heinemann Library, 2012)

Secrets of World War II (Top Secret Files), Sean McCollum (Raintree, 2017)

Spies and Code Breakers (Heroes of World War II), Claire Throp (Heinemann-Raintree, 2016)

World War II Visual Encyclopedia (DK History 10), DK (DK Children, 2015)

WEBSITES

www.bbc.co.uk/schools/primaryhistory/world_war2/world_at_war/
Learn all about the world at war at this BBC website.

www.ducksters.com/history/world_war_ii/
Check out this website to learn more about World War II, including spies and secret agents working during the war.

www.ww2escapelines.co.uk/?page_id=105
Learn more about the Comet Escape Line, and other World War II escape routes, at the WW2 Escape Lines Memorial Society website.

INDEX

TITLES IN THIS SET

BEHIND ENEMY LINES:
The Escape of Robert Grimes with the Comet Line

DEATH CAMP UPRISING:
The Escape from Sobibor Concentration Camp

OUTRUNNING THE NAZIS:
The Brave Escape of Resistance Fighter Sven Somme

TUNNELLING TO FREEDOM:
The Great Escape from Stalag Luft III